Switch-Pitcher

Marc J. Reilly

The Thieves Press

Cover Photo by betochagas/www.123rf.com

Printed in the United States of America

First Printing, 2019

ISBN 978-1-947107-12-0

The Thieves Press
www.crookbooks.site

Baseball is perhaps the most documented game in history. In this book I have attempted to inject a fictional character into these hallowed grounds. Actual players, living and dead, are mentioned, as are existing teams. Aware that many readers are as passionate about the game as I, my research was exhaustive and I made every effort to stay true to facts regarding real players or actual events. Any errors should immediately be taken as grains of salt, tossed over the shoulder for good luck, and the author promptly forgiven.

I would like to thank Bob Brenly. We have never met, but as a boy, I watched him behind the plate. I later listened to him announce the Diamondbacks' games. I cheered when he was made manager, and was over the moon when he led the team to a World Series Championship. I was saddened when he left for Chicago, and leapt for joy when he returned to Arizona to once again become the TV color analyst for the D-backs.

When Mr. Brenly speaks, I listen. Even when my team is outmatched, I remain glued to the TV because he is in the booth. For those not lucky enough to hear him do his job, let me explain. He does more than just announce, or add interesting statistics and baseball trivia. Every single game, he unselfishly gives an insider's view of the sport, play by play. He enlightens those who want to know what's really going on behind the scenes. If a listener is a newbie, he explains the game so anyone can understand the beauty of it. For seasoned fans, "BB" pulls back the curtain and shows us the magician's tricks.

I have learned more about baseball by listening to him than all the books I've read, research I've done, and players I've interviewed. It is an absolute certainty this story would not be what it is without the knowledge I gleaned from him.

Many thanks also to Greg A. Harris and Pat Venditte for being switch-pitchers and changing the game of baseball.

Books by Marc J. Reilly

<u>Tinman Series</u>

Posse of Thieves

Shady Deal

Calling the Shots

<u>Coming Soon</u>

Nut Job

<u>Tinman Special Releases</u>

Thieves Cookbook

Real Crooks Do Eat Quiche

By Cook or By Crook

Thieves Recipes

<u>Other</u>

Love on the Lam

Switch-Pitcher

To Peg, who insisted Gil's story be told once and for all.

Top of the 1st

I'M NOT SURE WHY I'M DOING THIS, but my mom bought me this little book, and there's nothing in it but blank pages. She said if I'm planning on being famous, WHICH I AM, then someday, people will want to read about my life. I know I'll never read it, because I'll already know what happens. Anyway, this book has got a lock on it with a little key, which is kinda stupid, cause anybody could rip it right off if they wanted to look inside. Not sure why anyone would do that, but I'll use the lock anyway, because it's there, and I'll keep the key someplace safe.

My mom says this is called a diary. But I didn't like that, because it sounds like something a girl would have. So she suggested I call it my journal. Well, I thought she said journey. So I decided to call it, <u>MY JOURNEY TO STARDOM</u>, and wrote it right on the front. I added the bit about stardom, cause I figured it sounded more interesting. People say you shouldn't judge a book by its cover, but I do, so that's why I did it.

I guess the best place to begin is the beginning. My teacher says I'm not real smart, and I mostly believe her. But I figure even a smart person would think starting at the beginning was a good idea, so that's what I'll do. It'll take me awhile, because holding a pencil always makes my hand cramp, and I have to take frequent breaks. Also, my mom says if I don't know how to spell a word, I have to look it up in the dictionary she gave me last year. My teacher suggested she do that, because, as I said already, she don't think I'm too smart. And being a teacher she must know everything, RIGHT?

I'm actually pretty good at reading. I learned by reading the backs of baseball cards and game recaps in the newspaper and computer, not from any book my teacher gave me. I think that's why she thinks I'm dumb, because all I know is baseball. But that's all I want to know, so why should I read anything else? Makes sense to me.

Anyway, til now, I've lived what they call a charmed life. Anyone would think the same if they had six dads. Which sounds impossible, but I'll explain. My mom's real name is Alice, but everyone calls her Al. She prefers that. In fact, I heard she once broke a beer bottle over a guy's head for calling her Alice. Me, I just call her mom, except when she's in a bad mood, then privately I call her Ice, using the last three letters of her name, which I think is funny because it is. Course I would never call her that to her face, or she might bust something over my head. Anyway, she's a biker chick, and was married before I was around. All the boys in the club say her husband was a real jerk. He used to beat on her, and she didn't like that. Well, she told the boys about it, and they up and beat on him, real bad. Then they kicked him out of the club, and he left for parts unknown.

Well, after he was gone, my mom said she didn't want no more husbands. She just wanted one of me. A kid. And she said she was running out of time, given her age. Problem was, she still needed a man to get the job done. That's according to the rules of nature, as she put it when she first explained about sex and such. Well, she told the boys what she was after, and they all admire her, but not one of them was having anything to do with being married. Some already were, or had been, and the ones that hadn't were afraid she would change her mind after the deed was done. She assured them it was not part of her plan, she just needed one of their sperms. She told them she had even gone to what they call a sperm bank, but the cost of $500 a pop for something so simple and natural was way out of her reach.

She suggested that six of her favorites act as her private sperm bank, with each one donating a little for the cause. She said nobody would ever know who the dad was, because the donations would remain anonymous, and she would pick one at random. This way, no one would feel any obligation toward me. She promised to take care of raising me, and the boys would be off the hook. Well, the six Chosen Ones had little to argue with over such a clever plan, so they went ahead and deposited their contributions into the bank.

Now this next part is top secret, so maybe there is some point to this lock and key. Because my mom never told anyone but me that once she had these six donations in her sperm bank (the freezer in our kitchen) she was afraid to let anything go to chance. So over a period of a week, once a night, she took a donation and did whatever women do with such things. (I don't know the details and I don't want to!) Anyway, by Sunday of that week she had used up every single bottle and was certain one of them sperms had done the trick.

Sure enough, nine months later, I popped out, and mom named me, Gil. Now, I know she named me after the goofy guy on Gilligan's Island. She's crazy for that show and is always watching the reruns. But I decided I'm named after Gil Hodges. I'm no first baseman, but it's best to be named after a great ballplayer than a doofus who got himself stuck on an island and never even tries to make out with Ginger or Mary Ann!

Now, some of you might think what my mom did is downright whacko. But I don't see it that way. Not one of the boys thinks so either. In fact if they were to hear anyone speak different, well, might just find that body out in the desert past Iron Springs Road someday. Yeah, my mom's a good woman. And she's real practical. She had a goal, and found a way to make it happen despite all difficulties.

One thing she didn't count on, was after I came out, all the boys who participated in the plan became attached to the idea of being a dad, despite none of them knowing who it was. So, they all just started assuming the role. The rest of the boys in the club also help out keeping an eye over me. I figure they're like my uncles. Course, they're not the sorts to cramp my style any. Much of the time, they're out with their hogs anyway. Sometimes I think they love them damn things more than me or my mom.

But when they're not messing around with the hogs, or doing club business, they're settled in at the clubhouse and they don't mind at all that I hang around. They say I make them laugh. Which is to be expected, on account of I'm just naturally funny. I've heard a lot about the boys and what their business is, and there is no denying they are some bad hombres. And my mom says despite one of them being my dad, she doesn't want me becoming like them. In fact, after I was born, she kinda wasn't a biker chick anymore. She settled in and has only one thing on her mind, taking care of me. I tell her she has no need to worry about me being part of a biker gang. I couldn't give a damn about hogs or patches or whatever their business is. And behind all the leather and the grizzle, I think they're just boys who aren't sure how to fit in. But that's their problem, not mine. For now, I just use them for my purposes, which I'll explain in a bit.

As you can see, my life has been real charmed. I like my town, most of the time. There are only a few hundred living here, and you can learn everybody's name in under a week. Took me longer than that, but that's because I'm not too smart, remember? And don't let the name fool you. People hear Skull Valley and figure it must be a dump. All desert, no trees. But it's not like that. Our teacher, Miss Smartypants, told us the name came from the white people who first showed up and found all these skulls from the Indians doing battle among themselves. Turns out, Skull Valley could be a real good place to grow things and the Indians fought over the right to do that. I guess they killed themselves off over it, because when these white people showed up, all they found were bones. And that's how it got its name. Not because it's ugly or nothing. Heck, right time of the year, we got the greatest creek ever. And there are big cottonwoods, and Mr. Miller across the way has sheep and fields growing all sorts of things. I'm glad it's not the desert. I need green to make me happy. And there's plenty of that.

The only thing that makes my town the pits is the lack of kids. Not that I'm crazy for kids, but it'd sure be nice to have enough to get a decent ballgame together. As it is, I got my best friend Tucker who's an okay catcher, and the Wilson sisters do alright in the outfield. Then there's little Tim, but he's too young to do much but cover first. On occasion, some kids come out of Prescott to visit their other parent, and we can fill the infield. But there's just not enough to go around to make up a second team.

This is real frustrating to me, because I'm planning on being a Hall of Fame pitcher. And it gets <u>DAMN</u> hard to practice when you can't get up a proper game. But I shouldn't whine. This is where my dads and uncles become useful. They make sure I get plenty of practice. None of them are too good, but they built me a mound behind the clubhouse so I can get the feel of pitching up high, like the king of the hill I aim to be. Problem is, most of the time, the boys have been drinking beer and it gets real easy to strike them out. Even when I throw garbage they just can't lay off. Still, I appreciate them for trying and giving me the practice I need to be a star.

Now I was born a righty, but I learned early on lefties have a natural advantage, so that's what I became. Grab whatever edge you can. But I do most everything else with my right. My favorite team is the Diamondbacks. Have to be, Arizona bred and all. And I just know someday they'll be <u>BEGGING</u> me to play for them. That's a promise.

My mom says when I get old enough, she's going to put me in the high school up at Prescott so I can play proper games. Until then, I'll just make do with what I have. There's no point in complaining. I got the best life a kid could want, with all the love and support the boys and mom can give. I thank my stars I could be so lucky. Well, I have to go now. I have a new pitch I want to try out. I guess I'll get back to this at some point. Though I'm not sure why it's important. I've just learned to trust in my mom the way she trusts in me. She's as certain as I am that I will be famous someday. And as much as I want it for myself, I would never let that woman down. Just like her, I'll find a way to reach my goal. <u>NO MATTER WHAT</u>.

Chapter 1

GIL HAYES CLOSED HIS JOURNAL, flipped the leather hasp over the top and with a little squeeze, engaged the lock. He stood up from his writing desk and looked around for a proper hiding spot. There weren't many options. His was the second bedroom in a single-wide mobile home, circa 1972. The walls were paneled in old-fashioned wooden laminate, but there wasn't much visible with all the posters of baseball players and other memorabilia. His single bed was tucked in the corner under the one window, a stack of baseball instructional books next to it.

Across from it was a writing desk that had been salvaged from the elementary school when they replaced theirs. Next to the hallway door, was his closet, the doors missing because they had long ago fallen out of their slides, and neither Gil nor Alice knew how to fix them. On the back of the hallway door hung a full-size newspaper foldout of Randy Johnson sneering out at home plate, preparing to crucify the next batter. The picture was featured in the AZ Republic during the 2001 World Series against the Yankees. Gil had watched it when he was six years old, and it was the inspiration for him to want to be a pitcher.

The drawer of his desk was filled with baseball cards, and scorecards. The blanket on his bed was black felt embellished with teal and purple rattlesnake heads, the logo for the Diamondbacks.

Noticeably missing for a boy his age were video games. And no TV. There was only the one in the living room, where he and Alice watched the ballgames. He did have a battery-powered radio on his desk for when the power went out—a frequent occurrence in Podunk Skull Valley. In such cases, he would listen to "The Governor" and "Candy Man" Candiotti call the game on radio.

Gil's eyes scoured the tiny space, searching. He loved his room. Just like he loved just about everything life tossed at him. He didn't need much, and he didn't have much. Which worked out just fine. The way he figured it, if a person had too many things, it took their mind off of what was important.

An idea came and he grabbed his desk chair and moved it under the ceiling light with a frosted glass shade. He never used the light, because it didn't work. Yet another thing neither he nor Alice knew how to fix. He had a small gooseneck lamp on his desk, and for nighttime reading, a flashlight by his bed. He reached up high and slid the journal on top of the shade.

Satisfied, he hopped down, knowing his secrets were safe. Despite his mom being a former, hard-nosed biker chick, she stood only 5' 2" and Gil knew she would never be able to see the journal so high up. For this purpose her diminutive size was a good thing, but otherwise, it bothered him no little. He turned thirteen in March, and still stood a hair under her. He kept hoping for a growth spurt, and prayed nightly that whoever's sperm was responsible for him came from one of the tall dads. Pitchers were always tall, and for his dream to come true, he would need to be, as well.

He stepped to his closet and reached up on the shelf where he kept a variety of colored sacks and balls. He chose three and stood over his bed. This was an essential part of his warm-up routine before he pitched. He'd once read that juggling helped develop the brain functions, and improved hand-eye coordination. Alice, always eager to assist, bought him, Juggling for Dummies.

Within a month, he no longer needed the book. He was a natural, quickly mastering cascade juggling, and moving on to bounce juggling using a wall as the point of contact. Then came shower juggling where the balls go around in a circle. He was now working on contact juggling where he would bounce one of the falling balls on his knee or elbow before returning it to the cascade.

For Gil, there was no better activity to get him in the zone. The brain had no choice but to concentrate completely on keeping the floating objects aloft. The enemy was gravity, never sleeping, never losing focus, always intent on winning. He felt great satisfaction in beating it.

As he juggled, he counted out the number of rotations without a sack or ball hitting the ground. He was at a level now, that unless he was trying some new maneuver, he could go until his arms gave out without gravity winning.

After twenty minutes of practice, he replaced the sacks in the closet and stepped into the hallway. Noon was still an hour away, but it was already hot. He thought about turning on the swamp cooler, but decided it was pointless to cool an empty house. Soon he and Alice would be gone for the day.

He could hear his mom in her bedroom, frantically getting ready for work. She worked in Kirkland, the next town over, and Gil had never known her to be ahead of schedule. The owner of the bar and grill, however, had the hots for her and didn't complain over her tardiness.

He moved quickly to the small, but tidy kitchen. He opened the refrigerator and removed the fixings for a grilled ham and cheese sandwich. Due to his mother's schedule, he fended for himself most of the time, and was a decent hand in the kitchen, regularly preparing meals for both of them.

He heard his mom's door open and called, "You want a sandwich before you go?"

"No time!" she said, rushing into the bathroom. "What have you been up to all morning? I haven't heard a peep? I thought you'd gone out."

Gil swirled the butter in the bottom of the pan, then laid his sandwich in and put a lid over it. "I been writing in that little book you gave me."

Alice appeared in the doorway, smoothing back her cropped brown hair. She was indeed a little thing, with her weight aptly matching her shortness. One would be hard pressed to imagine her as a biker chick, but for the myriad tattoos.

"Oh yeah?" she asked with a bemused grin. "Can I read it when I get home?"

"No, mom, you sure can't. That books secret. Why do you think they put a lock and key on it. Just for show?"

She chuckled. "Did you like what you wrote?"

"Sure. A real masterpiece of literature. And I spelled everything right. But it took me all damn morning and my hand feels like it's crippled for life."

She tousled his hair. He grudgingly let her, rolling his eyes, however, in consternation. She laughed and whacked his butt. "I've got to work a double, so you're on your own for dinner."

"Again? You the only waitress they got?" asked Gil, expertly flipping his sandwich.

"Seems like it. That new girl only lasted two days."

"Probably couldn't handle Mr. Gropey. He better not do that stuff with you."

"I told you before, he does not grope me."

"No. He just undresses you with his eyes. And don't tell me otherwise, I seen it."

She shrugged. "No harm done, if that's how he gets his kicks. At least I got a job. Look, I gotta run."

"You take this sandwich. I'll make another one." She frowned at him. "Don't argue with me, mom." He removed the sandwich and wrapped it in a paper towel.

"You know I get an employee discount for my shift meal."

"All that place shovels out is slop. And you'll have to suffer through it for dinner. At least you'll have a good lunch." He handed her the sandwich, and her lips trembled as she glowed at him.

"God sure gave me a good turn when he gave me you."

"Don't be going and giving him all the credit! I expect it was mostly dumb luck."

She guffawed as only Alice could do, then kissed him on the cheek and spun for the front door. "Be good!"

"Don't expect miracles. And don't drive too fast!" The screen door slammed shut and he retrieved the fixings for another sandwich. He heard their old heap of junk struggle to life, then the sound of the engine faded in the distance.

After his early lunch, he grabbed his mitt and glove and headed out. Their trailer was the first on Copper Basin Road, right across from the railroad tracks. The train came once or twice a week, and it was the only entertainment besides what a kid can come up with on his own.

The town consisted of: The General Store, built in 1916; The Garage, boasting two gas pumps that would look good in an antique store; The School, grades 1-8, with two teachers and thirty students in a good year; The Volunteer Fire Station; and The Post Office, open three days a week.

That was it. Skull Valley was a throwback, belonging in a time that no longer existed. The modern world having passed it over.

Most Sundays, Gil worked stocking shelves in The General Store. The owner didn't need the help, because there were only a half dozen shelves. But he was a baseball fan, and knew Gil's earnings went solely to pay for the internet which he used to look up player statistics, and the cable fee so he could watch the games. Without them, Skull Valley would have been intolerable.

But, today was a Saturday and he had the day to himself. Better yet, there was only a week left of school before summer break. Next semester he'd be in 8th grade, but that was a long time off. Life was looking good. He knew it was too early to head to the clubhouse. The boys wouldn't be awake from their Friday festivities yet, and even if they were, it was always best to wait for them to start cranking back beers to chase away the evening's hangovers.

He crossed over Iron Springs Road, en route to the creek. He knew he'd find Tucker there, and wasn't disappointed.

Tucker liked baseball okay, but he was no fanatic like Gil. Fishing was his thing, and there he was, rod in hand. What they called the creek was actually a wash. Like baseball, it only ran part of the year, fueled by the snowmelt from the Bradshaw Mountains. But when it did, it was as glorious a creek as ever there was. Water is precious in the high desert, and the very sight of it brought hope for better things.

Gil had rarely seen Tucker catch a fish from the creek, but that didn't deter him. They shared that understanding. If one was just tenacious and pigheaded enough, one would eventually succeed. No matter what the odds.

"Tuckaroo!"

"Sshhhh. I think I felt a nibble," whispered Tucker.

Gil walked on cat's feet until he reached the bank, then huddled next to his friend. After a few minutes, however, a shrug from Tucker indicated that, yet again, it was merely a false hope.

"Too late in the day for them to be biting," said Gil.

"Don't I know it," said Tucker casting his line again.

The two sat amicably, neither willing to break the calmness of the day with idle chatter. The air was filled with little cotton wisps from the shedding cottonwood overhead. Gil worked his baseball, trying out different grips while Tucker focused intently on the still water.

Out of the blue, Tucker said, "My mom said I can't go to the clubhouse anymore."

"She's a broken record," answered Gil. "You eat yet?"

"Sure."

"We'll head up in about an hour. Boys should be cranking them back by then."

"Sure."

Gil laid on his back and idly tossed the ball in the air, catching it inches from his face. The two could have been twins, with the same height and weight. The only difference was Tucker's hair was sandy, and Gil's dark, like his mom's.

"I'm going to try out a new pitch today."

Tucker shot him a look. "Why would you do that?"

13

"So I have a new pitch! Why else?"

"You're best sticking to them sliders and curveballs. That's what you're good at."

"I need a fastball to set up the breaking balls! Pitching 101."

Tucker pulled out two pieces of gum and flipped one to Gil. "You've been practicing this new pitch of yours?"

"Course not! That's why I said it's a new pitch."

"And you want to try it out at the clubhouse."

"Where else am I gonna try it out?" said Gil, popping his bubble with a loud crack. "What's gotten into you?"

"Nothing. Just a fastball is a lot faster than other pitches. You sure you can spot it?"

"No I ain't sure! That's what practice is all about. Come on, let's get a move on."

Tucker stashed his rod in its normal hiding spot, and they wandered away from the creek, mitts in hand. Tucker also carried his catcher's mask which was a recent acquisition after one of Gil's sliders took a funny bounce and landed on his nose. After that, his mother—not a fan of baseball—finally succumbed and bought him a $20 cheapie at the Prescott Walmart for his birthday. She still refused, however, to buy him a catcher's mitt, not understanding the need. So Tucker caught with a normal outfielder's mitt, but still, he was grateful for small mercies—and no more bloody noses.

When they reached Copper Basin Road, they took a quick pit stop at Gil's house so he could make a sandwich for Tucker, who he knew full well was lying about having eaten already. Tucker's mom was stingy with everything, including food.

Back on Copper Basin Road, Gil handed Tucker his mitt. Tucker walked ahead some distance while Gil waited.

Long ago, he had marked out a stretch of the road that measured exactly sixty yards. When Tucker reached that point, he held up an arm. Gil prepared himself, bending his knees slightly and hunching over. Tucker dropped his arm, and Gil shot off.

He was a true student of the game of baseball, and was always looking for an edge. He noticed pitchers never tried to run fast. He was determined to be different. From a young age, he began building an arsenal of weapons that would make him an invaluable member for any team.

He raced past Tucker who had been counting off the seconds. He jogged back, and said, "Well?"

"I take it as 8.5. But I'm no stopwatch, like I keep telling you."

"Let me try again." Gil trotted back to the starting line. He was not a perfectionist, he just knew when he could do better. Case in point: he openly admitted he was not a good hitter. His bat speed was too slow and he didn't have enough bulk on his body. But that didn't stop him from learning how to handle a bat. It's just that he only specialized in one kind of hit. The bunt. And he was very, very good at it.

He'd once heard Bob "BB" Brenly, former manager of the D-backs and currently a television color analyst, complaining how pitchers didn't learn how to bunt. He swore it was an invaluable skill, and they were missing a beat.

Gil filed that bit of information away. Initially, however, his skills at bunting came about as a form of self-defense. On days at the clubhouse when he had struck out every man standing, the boys would often demand a crack at striking him out. None of them could pitch real well, and Gil found his only protection was bunting the ball. After that, he practiced until he could bunt damn near any pitch that came at him. The only exception was the 12-6 curveball. Because of his slow bat speed, that particular pitch was one that if he caught up to it, he could really whack. He didn't tell many people about it, as he considered it his secret weapon.

Gil got into his stance, and Tucker dropped his arm. Gil leapt forward and burned up the road. As he passed Tucker, his friend let out a whoop. Gil turned to him, panting.

"Eight flat!" cried Tucker. "And I'm damn sure of that." Gil smiled, and Tucker grinned back. "You'll get it down to under seven someday. I swear you will."

Gil slapped him on the back and they walked on, reaching where the thin macadam turned to gravel. Up ahead and to the right sat a plain clapboard house, off back by itself. Nothing really distinguished it from the other houses in Skull Valley except for the fleet of gleaming Harley Davidsons parked outside.

"I hope they're not too hammered," said Tucker.

"Me too," said Gil. "It's too easy to strike them out. Where's the challenge in that?"

Chapter 2

"LOOKS LIKE A FULL HOUSE," said Tucker.

Gil shrugged, and they continued up the drive past the bikes. Most of the boys lived elsewhere, Chino Valley, Prescott, Wilhoit, even as far away as Congress and Bagdad. But on weekends, the members would gather on Friday night and stay until Sunday.

Gil and Tucker did not approach the front door, instead walking around to the back. A concrete block extension had been built on, conspicuous for the lack of windows. The boys said the add-on room was for the pool table, but Gil had no proof of this, as neither he nor Tucker had ever ventured inside. They didn't mind hanging outside with the gang, but they had no desire to know what they were up to inside.

At the far corner of the clubhouse, a beefy man with long, greasy, black hair was relieving himself against the wall. Gil noticed his 'cut,' or leather vest, did not have any patches. He knew this meant the man was a 'hang-around.' Not officially part of the club, he was not allowed to wear any patches until he went through the exhaustive process of recruitment and initiation. It could take up to two years before he was finally 'patched in,' and became a full-fledged member.

Gil thought it a ridiculously long process to get to wear a few patches and be part of a club, but to each his own. As he and Tucker walked out to the pitching mound, the man spied them.

"Hey! What are you two punks doing around here. Get the hell back home." He zipped up and stepped threateningly toward them.

"You don't want to do that," said Gil matter-of-factly.

"Oh, yeah?! What you gonna do? Hurt me?"

"Nah. The boys will take care of that."

The man paused midstep, suddenly unsure of the turf he was treading.

Gil tossed the ball idly up and down. "Just go on in there and tell them Gil is here."

The man narrowed his eyes, and Gil instinctively didn't like him. His brain seemed not too sharp, which can be a dangerous thing when it's sitting on top of a 250 lb. hulking body. "We'll see," said the man. With all the strut and bravado he could muster he sauntered toward the back door.

"Man, I sure wish we had regular kids to play ball with," said Tucker. "Not these drunken fools."

"It'll be better someday," said Gil. "Once we get to Prescott."

"Hell, my mom will never move there."

"We'll see," said Gil. "Let's get set up."

They walked to the back stoop where Gil grabbed a small rake and Tucker picked up a can of white spray paint. While Gil cleaned up his mound, Tucker resprayed the square representing home plate. Once satisfied, they took their positions.

Gil said, "If I wipe my face, it means I want to throw the fastball, a four-seamer."

Tucker sighed heavily, and pulled down his mask. Gil pitched several balls and was feeling the juice in his arm when the backdoor slammed open and "Jawbones," one of his dads, came barreling out.

"G-Man! And Tuckeroo! How you boys doing?"

"Peachy keen, Jawbones," said Gil.

Much like baseball players, all the boys had nicknames. Gil had been dubbed, "G-Man" by another one of his dads, "Roadkill," who thought it sounded like some sort of superhero. Gil didn't mind, and always answered to it.

Within a minute, twenty gnarly men bustled out. Grabbing folding chairs they lined either side of home plate, the concrete back wall functioning as the backstop.

Several of them carried baseball bats. Gil knew they owned them for more sinister reasons than playing ball, but he didn't pry. He didn't want to know.

In the unlikely event anyone hit a ball off Gil, two guys were stationed on lawn chairs out in left and right field. As the boys worked out the batting line-up, a couple of their lady friends dutifully hauled out a cooler full of beer. When everyone was settled in, the first man stepped up to the plate, and the contest began.

Gil knew the routine. The boys wouldn't get serious until he had racked up a lot of strikeouts. Until then, it would just be a lark, a way to entertain themselves and loll away an hour or two on a hot Saturday. But if he could keep striking them out, they would get irked and try harder. And that's precisely what he did.

In quick succession, he struck out "Cueball," "Bear," "Sasquatch," "Mutant," and "Rooster." He fed them a steady diet of sliders and curveballs. Just like Tucker said, it's what he was good at. The victims received boisterous catcalls and jeers. The two men in the outfield announced they were falling asleep and needed some action.

"Coyote" grabbed a bat, and Gil knew this was his first real competition. Tucker called for a slider inside and Gil nodded. The pitch hung a little, and Coyote clipped it sending it high and just foul. His mates cheered him on. Tucker called for the same pitch and this time Gil got it right. The ball released off the index finger with the correct pressure, and was a real snapper, breaking hard inside like a bowling ball sinker should. Coyote's bat whistled through the air several inches above the ball. Strike two.

Tucker called for the same pitch, thinking Coyote wouldn't expect three in a row, but Gil shook it off. He knew Coyote was onto him. Tucker changed to a splitter, a pitch Gil rarely threw, but he liked the call. He nestled the ball in his mitt to hide the split grip of his index and middle fingers. He calmed his mind, knowing to make the pitch correctly, he needed to force the hand and forearm down at the end of his motion to reduce the backspin. He went into his windup and came over the top, hurling the ball forward. Coyote grinned, sensing a hanging ball. But just before it crossed the plate, it dropped off the table and slapped into Tucker's mitt. Coyote had swung way over top, and slammed his bat on the ground.

Gil could sense the onlookers were growing restless. Now they actually wanted to hit the ball. No more fooling around. Things took on an edge of seriousness as "Torpedo" grabbed a bat.

Gil was unmoved. Torpedo was a free swinger and would go after nearly anything that was remotely close to the plate. Tucker also knew the routine and gave Gil a little grin through his mask. The first pitch was an outside sinker and it nearly turned Torpedo around as he flailed at it. The audience grumbled. Gil accepted the call of 12-6 curveball from Tucker, and if it were not for the angry grimace on Torpedo after he swung a mile over top, the results would have been comical. The third pitch was a slurve—the grip the same as a curve but thrown with the velocity of a slider. The result was indescribable and devastating to the batter. Torpedo yowled and his friends moaned.

After that, it seemed as if the boys had lost heart. No one was willing to try their hand, and Gil was just getting warmed up. Someone suggested they move to the pool table, and it appeared as if the game was going to be called.

Right then, the new guy Gil and Tucker had met when they first showed up, said he would give it a try. Everyone knew he was just trying to impress, hoping it would help him in his cause to become a member. "Balrog," another of Gil's dads and de facto leader of the local clubhouse, waved him up to the plate. It appeared as if he didn't yet merit a nickname, but privately Gil was referring to him as "Greasy."

He grabbed a bat and strutted up. "You met your match, little man. I played plenty of ball when I was your age. My specialty was making pitchers cry."

Gil was too seasoned to let the needling get to him. He stared in at Tucker who dropped two fingers, very slowly. Gil nodded. He knew what he was after. A lazy curveball should show this fool up. He went into his windup and threw, the ball did what it was supposed to, but Greasy just stood there watching it hit the dirt a good three feet before the plate and roll into Tucker's mitt.

"You ain't gonna fool me," said Greasy. "I been watching. I know what you got."

Gil turned and spat. It was going to take something special. Maybe another slurve. Tucker was of the same mind and dropped down the sign. Gil stepped back, putting on the proper grip. But the moment the ball was released from his hand, he knew it had slipped. Instead of breaking down and away, it drifted up and up, until Greasy shot out a hand and caught it at eye-level.

"Way up and out! Ball two. How about trying that splitter you got. I bet I can hit it to the Bradshaws." He flung the ball back to the mound.

None of the boys had seen this kind of treatment to Gil's pitching, and they were grudgingly impressed. Still, there were scattered cheers for their ace, hoping he could put the newbie in his place.

Gil stepped off the mound and wiped his face. He looked to see if Tucker had spotted it. He had, but instead of hunkering into position, he called time, and came jogging out, shaking his head. He huddled up with Gil.

"This ain't the time or place to be trying something new."

"I'm not going to let this guy off the hook," said Gil angrily.

"Did I say you should? Just come inside with the slider. Tie him into knots."

Gil looked away, breathing heavily. "You my catcher or not?"

Tucker furrowed his brow. "You know I am."

"Then get ready for the four-seamer, like I called."

Tucker sighed heavily. "Christ. How will I even know where it's going?"

"High and tight. We'll chase him off the plate, then next pitch we slide out and away. After that, he won't know what's coming."

Tucker stared evenly at Gil who met his eyes. The boys started jeering, calling for the continuation of play. Greasy just stood and laughed, looking out at the mound. Gil patted Tucker on the back, and he jogged back to the plate.

Gil had been practicing the grip for the four-seamer for some time. He'd thrown several at the tree in his backyard. He felt confident he could spot it in the position he wanted. The key was to let the ball leave the thumb at the top of his motion, with the index and middle finger rolling down the back of the ball to give the correct amount of backspin. Optimally, it should have no break whatsoever.

"Come over the top," Gil whispered to himself as he went into his windup. The release felt perfect. The ball sailed forward, faster than any of his other pitches. It seemed up to the last moment as if it would find it's spot. But it started drifting, too far inside, until the outcome became painfully obvious.

The ball smacked Greasy hard in the left shoulder then caromed off the tip of his head. For a moment there was absolute silence. No one had ever been hit by one of Gil's pitches, and it seemed almost like an illusion.

Greasy knew otherwise. He bellowed, then let out a curse of profanity no thirteen-year-old boy should hear. Before anyone could react he started toward the mound. Tucker instinctively sprang from his crouch and grabbed his legs, but Greasy kicked out, landing a heavy boot on his mask, sending him crashing backward.

Halfway to the mound, Greasy picked up speed, his bat curled over his shoulder, aiming to hit a homerun with Gil's head. Gil held his ground, not out of courage, but confusion. He'd never been in this position before.

"Now we'll see if I can hit you!" cried Greasy. He swung, and Gil dropped to the ground just in time to hear the whistle of the bat as it sped over his head. He knew Greasy was not finished and covered his face.

There was an eruption of noise as the boys cleared the bench. Greasy tried to run, but it was twenty to one. They surrounded him, fists flying, bats jabbing. Gil peeked out and for a strange moment his mind went back to the previous summer. He and Tucker had been at the creek when they saw the strangest thing. A young female duck had apparently committed some terrible crime and the other ducks, mostly male, were attacking it, poking viciously at its head, trying to hold it under water and drown it. Neither he nor Tucker could ever figure out what a little duck could have done to deserve such treatment.

He scrambled to his feet and heard his voice yelling, "It was me! The ball just got away. He didn't do nothing!"

His pleas were drowned out by the ferocity of the gang's attack. Greasy was already bleeding from the nose and had ceased fighting back. But Jawbones grabbed his vest, held him steady and released a terrible undercut catching him square on the jaw. His head snapped back and he toppled, collapsing right on top of Gil.

Gil heard a crack, and wondered where it had come from. It was not the sound of bat on ball. He looked to his left arm, and saw it was bent a little funny at the elbow. He reached for it with his right hand and tried to straighten it. The pain sliced through him like a saber thrusting up from his belly to his brain. He faded away, his scream lingering like a half-remembered dream.

Chapter 3

GIL FELT HIMSELF RISING, and wondered if he was going to heaven. But the pain in his arm was so severe, he figured he must still be alive. He was highly skeptical about there being an Almighty, but if there was, it would only make sense he or she or it would not allow hurt to exist after you're dead. What would be the point in that? It's supposed to be heaven, for God's sakes.

He opened his eyes to reality and saw the boys huddled around, staring in horror. He had never seen any of them look so scared over anything. He realized he was in Jawbones' arms, and the big brute had tears bubbling up.

"We gotta make a sling!" cried someone. "Get some sticks for splints, and we need some cloth."

There was some hurried activity as Jawbones slowly carried Gil to the front of the house. Tucker appeared, looking worried. "Here, use my shirt."

Jawbones placed Gil on the seat of one of the hogs. "This is gonna hurt, buddy," he said, voice trembling. "But it's gotta be done."

Gently, he lifted Gil's injured arm. Roadkill placed two wooden shims on top and bottom. Balrog tore Tucker's shirt in two and used one half to wrap the shims in place. He draped the other piece over Gil's shoulder, tying it below the elbow, forming a makeshift sling. Gil clamped his teeth to force back the screams begging to be released.

"Let's go!" said Balrog. "He'll ride with me."

"The hell he will!" cried Jawbones. "He's mine."

"Alright then," said Balrog. "The rest of you, form a convoy. Two on all sides. Schizo and Blade, you take point. Clear the way. I don't want nothing stopping us until we hit Prescott. We go straight to the ER."

The air suddenly exploded with angry thunder as the gang fired up their bikes. Jawbones nestled Gil in front of him over the gas tank, and everyone pulled out. By the time they reached Iron Springs Road, Jawbones' bike was surrounded by an armada of speeding hogs. Schizo and Blade ran a half mile in front, tearing up the road, drawing out any cops that might be hiding.

They raced across the flats, and soon the elevation began to rise as they turned east toward the Bradshaws. Despite the excruciating pain, Gil felt a little thrill wash over him. All the time he had hung out with the boys, he had never ridden on one of their bikes. He wished it was under different circumstances.

They encountered few cars. The few going in the same direction, they forced over to the side and raced past. Ones coming at them simply pulled over, as there was no available lane.

When they passed the turnoff to Little Granite Mountain, Gil knew they more than halfway there. By the time they reached Black Jack Spring he was shivering and couldn't understand why, given the heat of the day.

Jawbones sensed it. He leaned in and asked, "Can you move your fingers?"

Gil tried, and found he could. "Yeah, but it hurts like hell."

"I'm so sorry G-Man."

"Not your fault, dammit. I shouldn't've tried the fastball. Tucker warned me."

Jawbones laughed nervously, but his eyes were still blurry and wet. The gang roared into Prescott, oblivious to the stares and pointing. They pulled into the ER nineteen minutes after having left the clubhouse. A record time. Balrog ordered the gang to wait outside. He didn't want to scare the hospital staff and delay treatment for Gil. He instructed Mutant and Toxin to ride to Kirkwood and forewarn Alice what had befallen. It was an unenviable task, and the others watched them go, thanking their lucky stars they had not been chosen. Balrog and Jawbones started for the front entrance, but Gil's other dads, Roadkill, Diablo, Satyr and Knuckles, demanded they accompany them. Leader or no, there was little Balrog could do, and he consented.

The sun had long set before they reappeared. It was a tricky and serious fracture, occurring where the radius met the elbow joint. Gil had to be sedated so the doctor could set it back in place. Thankfully, he could remember little of the process. All he knew was his arm was now in a full cast, the elbow in a fixed bend. The doctor said it would be quite some time before it healed.

Gil's dads wanted to pay the hefty tab in cash, but despite their persuasive ways, the hospital said bills had to be sent out, and payment remitted in the official manner.

The drive back to Skull Valley was somber, made even more so when they reached the front yard of Gil and Alice's trailer. The bikes lined up out front, and the men dismounted. Mutant and Toxin were standing out front, eyes wide with trepidation.

The front door swung open and Alice stepped out. It was clear why in these kinds of moments, Gil referred to her as "Ice." She said not a word, her eyes slowly taking in each man, sending an unmistakable message.

Jawbones, with one hand on Gil's shoulder for protection, stepped forward. "Al, I take full responsibility."

She slapped him hard on the face. He hung his head, hoping for more to wipe away the guilt. But that was all that was forthcoming. She laid a hand on Gil's back and started him to the house.

"Mom, it wasn't their fault. I caused this!" cried Gil.

Suddenly, Alice's legs began to quiver. She sank to her knees and looked up at his cast. She ran a gentle finger down the length of it, tears pouring out. "Dammit, Gil. It's your throwing arm. What are you going to do now?"

"It's alright mom. It'll heal. I'll be as good as new, you'll see."

Balrog stepped up. He reached out to touch Alice on the shoulder, but thought better of it. "Al, they wouldn't let us pay at the hospital. But the bills are coming. Sure as hell." He bent down and laid some cash beside her. Without any prodding, each man stepped forward and fattened the stack.

When they had all left, Gil helped Alice to her feet with his good arm. He nudged her to the door, then scooped up the cash. Inside, she collapsed on the sofa, and Gil nestled next to her. It was going to be a long night.

It was nearing midnight before he could get her to bed. She was so distraught, she didn't even want to hear exactly what had happened. That could wait until another time. After she was tucked away, Gil went to the kitchen and with one arm wrestled out some peanut butter and bread. He was famished, and the sharp pain in his arm had turned to a nonstop throb, keeping him from even considering sleep.

He took his snack to his room, sat on the edge of his bed, and nibbled. A heavy depression was sinking down on him, like heavy fog, and he didn't want to succumb, fearing if he did, he would never find his way back out. He couldn't even bring himself to look at his beloved posters, because he was afraid perhaps his dream had died that day.

A rap on his window sent a spark through him. He pulled back the curtain and saw Tucker staring back. He unlocked the window and Tucker lifted it, then slithered through the opening. They sat beside each other on the bed for several minutes, neither talking.

Tucker finally laid a hand on Gil's shoulder and said, "Look at this way, G-Man, you beaned a Hells Angel and lived to tell about it."

"Hell, he wasn't even part of the club. Just a hang-around."

Tucker winked at him. "I won't tell if you don't."

Strangely, Gil found this terribly funny. He started to giggle and it turned into full-blown laughter. Tucker joined in and the two rocked back and forth.

"I warned you not to throw that damn fastball!" cried Tucker.

"And I never listen to my catcher!"

They laughed even more, until it subsided into a healing calmness. They both flopped back on the bed.

"So what are we going to do now?" asked Tucker. "While the arm heals?"

"Well, I'm not going to sit around none. It's summer. Time to play ball. I guess I'll just teach my good arm how to pitch, until the other one comes around. At least I'll stay in practice."

Tucker thought about this for several moments. "Well, if you can get even halfway decent as a righty, when your left comes back, you could be a switch-pitcher. Wouldn't that be something."

Gil snorted. "There's no such thing. Wouldn't even be legal."

"You just keep thinking that, and meanwhile, I'll bet you that Greg Maddux card of yours I'm right."

"You're serious aren't you?"

"Yup. Catchers are never wrong. Neither are best friends." He rolled his head to the side and smiled at Gil. "By the way, can I sign your cast? I'd like to be the first."

In the early morning hours, still unable to sleep, Gil hit the computer and found that Tucker had indeed spoken the truth—barely. There had been four switch-pitchers in the early days of baseball. But in the modern era there had only been one who threw with both arms in an MLB regulation game. His name was Greg A. Harris.

He played for several teams, and had pitched a total of 703 career games. Amazingly, during all that time, he only got to switch-pitch in one inning. The game occurred in 1995 (which brought a grin to Gil, because it was the year he was born).

He was playing at home for the Montreal Expos. The opposing team was the Cincinnati Reds and they were up by six. It was the top of the ninth and Harris' coach gave him the go-ahead to switch. Gil figured it was probably because the Expos were terrible that season with only a few games to go.

Gil's eyes widened as he saw that the first man up had been none other than the great Reggie Sanders. Harris pitched righty and got him to ground out to short. A feat in and of itself. The next two batters he pitched lefty. He walked the first, then got the next man to top the ball in front of the plate and the catcher threw him out. The fourth man up was Bret Boone. Gil swallowed hard. Boone came from a renowned baseball family, and was a three-time All Star, and a two-time Silver Slugger.

Harris chose to switch back to his right, which made sense since Boone was a righty. Boone hit a dribbler to the mound and Harris threw him out at first. Gil let out a whoop. He had never imagined such a thing.

The Expos went on to lose the game, but history had been made. It was the only time in the 20th century a pitcher threw an inning from both sides, and it turned out to be the next to last game Harris would ever pitch.

What about his glove? He had to have used the same one, but how? Gil went back to his research and discovered Harris had a custom mitt made especially for his unique talents. It had two thumbs. A six-finger glove. Gil shook his head in wonderment.

He stood up and stretched his back, then walked into the kitchen and awkwardly poured himself a glass of milk. He returned to the computer and got back to work. Surely, there had to be someone who had followed in Harris' footsteps. And indeed there was. Pat Venditte. He was ten years older than Gil and, lo and behold, had just made baseball news by being drafted by the New York Yankees.

He attended Creighton University, and his coach would not let him switch-pitch his freshman year for fear it would turn the game into a "circus." Gil snorted. He was as much a baseball traditionalist as anyone, but if a guy has special talents, you have to let him use them.

His sophomore year, the coach relented, and Venditte earned a 3.02 ERA in 62⅔ innings. Very respectable. In his junior year, however, he posted a 1.85 ERA, with a streak of 43⅔ scoreless innings, and was voted Midwest Region Pitcher of the year. Gil was duly impressed. So were the Yankees who drafted him in the 45th round. But Venditte turned them down, and went back to finish school, saying he wanted to increase the velocity of his left arm, and add another pitch to his right.

Gil could hardly believe it. To be drafted and turn it down! But as he read on, he could see why Venditte had been right to wait. When he eventually signed, he was drafted in the 20th round and assigned to the Staten Island Yankees, Class-A ball. He was now a pro, and Gil felt sure he would quickly move up the ranks. He made a note to follow his career. He had found himself a new hero. Two in fact. But Venditte was an active player, an up-and-comer.

He leaned back and let the information sift through his mind, making sense of what he'd learned. Seeing how it affected him.

The thing that made the most impression was that Tony "Count" Mullane, one of the early 19th century switch-pitchers with 284 wins—27th on the all-time list— had suffered an injury to his right arm early in his career. Instead of quitting, he taught himself to pitch lefty. True determination. Gil liked that. Make something good out of a bad.

From that perspective, the broken arm might even be considered a stroke of good luck. After all, if it hadn't happened, he would never have turned to his right arm to pitch. Now he was forced to. If he could learn to do that, when the left healed, he would be a double threat, and on his way to being the best switch-pitcher the game had ever seen. He nodded his head once, firmly. His sights set.

Some might think this was undue optimism, or perhaps a wonderful facility to overlook reality. But that's what made Gil who he was, and what makes the great ones dream bigger dreams than normal people.

Bottom of the 2ⁿᵈ

IT'S BEEN A LONG TIME since I wrote in this little book. Mostly, because I forgot all about it. And also, because I lost it. Actually I didn't know I'd lost it because as I said I forgot about it. I only remembered when our landlord, Mr. Jenkins, found it in our old trailer down in Skull Valley. Seems the new tenants complained about that overhead light in my bedroom not working. Something mom and I never considered doing, since we didn't want to bother Mr. Jenkins for fear he'd raise the rent.

Anyway, while he was trying to fix it, he found my book and knew right off whose it was because of the title. He already knew about me becoming famous someday, and that's how he worked it out. He's still our landlord, because when we moved to Prescott he showed us an apartment he also owned. Seems he owns a lot of places. Which is a good thing, because it made moving here go smoother than we had expected. We just kept paying him rent, only for a different place. The way it went down was kind of in a rush, and it could have gone a lot worse.

I realize I'm getting ahead of myself because I just reread the first entry in this book and found I'd left out a lot since then. But I don't want to take forever writing this because I got a pitch I want to practice, so I'll sum it up so we can get to the present.

First off, I broke my left arm. It was my own stupid fault. But don't be too sad because it turned out to be a lucky thing. It made me go to my dominant arm and learn to pitch with that. The whole idea came from Tucker who knew there was such a thing as a switch-pitcher. His thinking was if I could learn to pitch with both arms then I could be a switch-pitcher too. I took to the idea right off, because there have only been a very few switch-pitchers in the history of the game, which makes it that much easier for me to become famous. Makes sense to me.

Anyway, it was a couple weeks after the accident when Tucker and I figured we'd go on up to the clubhouse and have the boys sign my cast. I'll never forget it. It was after supper and we started walking up the street when all of a sudden we saw the rarest sight you could see in little Skull Valley. A whole stream of vehicles was turning onto Copper Basin Road. Had to be twenty or more. In the front, were several County Sherriff cars, followed by a whole pack of big, black SUVs, almost like a funeral procession, which I guess in a way it was.

Two of these vehicles stopped at the end of the road right after where the railroad tracks cross over. They positioned themselves nose to nose so no one could get through without going off the road. The rest of the vehicles drove on past and we could tell right off they were headed for the clubhouse.

One of the SUVs slowed and a man opened his window and told us we should get back home. There was going to be trouble. Well, Tucker and me never thought once before cutting across Mr. Miller's fields so we could approach the clubhouse without being seen by these cops.

It was a Friday and the boys had a full crew gathered. We watched as the cars peeled off, surrounding the house and preventing any escape. All at once, the doors of all these vehicles swung open and it seemed like an army of cops sprang out, many of them dressed up like they were going to war. And in a way, I guess maybe that's what they thought. They stormed the clubhouse from all sides, busting in the front and back doors, and smashing in windows.

Tucker and I waited for the battle to begin, knowing the boys would not go down easy. But to our surprise, we heard not a single gunshot. And soon, the boys started filing out, most in handcuffs. I saw four of my dads, plus a bunch of my uncles. They were stuffed into the black SUVs, and not one put up much of a fight. I guess they knew the cops had them dead to rights.

Well, Tucker and me raced back to the road and waited. Not long after, we saw the vehicles coming our way. I tried to see inside the SUVs, hoping to get a glimpse of my dads, but the windows were tinted, and all I saw was my own reflection, standing there by the side of the road.

The raid became national news, even bigger than when the boys first opened their clubhouse. The charges ranged from illegal gun possession to drug dealing. Jawbones and Roadkill weren't arrested for some reason. I guess they didn't have enough evidence. It had to be that, because I'm damn sure those two were up to the same as the others. Some of my uncles got off as well, but after the raid, we didn't see any of them. They scattered like a bevy of quail, which was natural. But I miss them some. I know they were bad dudes, but they were my kin, so to speak.

Mom kind of freaked out after that. She was already upset with the boys over my arm being broken, even though it wasn't really their fault. But this thing with the cops put her over the edge. She was afraid anyone associated with the gang would be next. I told her she had nothing to worry about, but she wouldn't listen. In her mind, Skull Valley was finished, and we were moving to Prescott.

Now, I liked Skull Valley and all, but I had always wanted to be where there were more kids, so I figured the raid on the clubhouse turned out to be a lucky thing. At least for me and my mom, surely not for the boys. But as we were getting our things together to do the move it dawned on me I was going to lose Tucker.

Well, my mom and his mom were never friends, but my mom could see I was upset. So she went to Tucker's mom and tried to convince her to move to Prescott with us. But she would have nothing to do with it. Said it would be too expensive and didn't care what Tucker wanted.

It seemed there was nothing that could be done, and it was a sad day when we pulled out of town with Tucker waving goodbye, tears in both our eyes. But as things worked out, it happened we didn't have nothing to worry about. The very next day, he showed up at our apartment. He had run away, and hitched a ride to the city. I told my mom we should just lay low, and his mom would never know where he was. But she couldn't do that. She called Tucker's mom and told her where her son was.

Well, it surprised her (but not Tucker or me because we knew his mom better) when she said if Tucker didn't want to live with her, that was fine by her. It would be cheaper. My mom got real upset with her, but she stuck to her guns. She said if my mom would put him up, she would send regular money to help support him. We knew she wouldn't, so it came as no surprise when she didn't. I thought my mom would send Tucker back, but she just accepted him like he was my brother. Which of course he is.

And Tucker just loves my mom for what she did. He became so concerned about the money he went right out and got a part-time job cleaning up at a garage down the street. The head mechanic even lets him help with little jobs, and says he's got the knack. Tucker gives every dime he makes to my mom to help with the added expenses he brings. And I got a job at a diner a few blocks away, cleaning up and doing a little prep work. I like being around food. Seems like I understand it more than most things. Mom's waiting tables again, but this new place is more upscale and she's doing alright with tips. I guess she likes it. She never complains.

Like the trailer, our apartment has just the two bedrooms, and Tucker and I share one, which is okay by us. My mom always says we get along like two peas in a pod and she's right. I miss the trailer, though. It had a yard where I could practice. This place has a field across the street, and Tucker and I have claimed it for our own. But it's still different, not really being ours. Also, the walls of this apartment are so thin I can follow the lives of our neighbors like a soap opera. Which is no treat, believe me!

But, all in all, it was a good move, and one that needed to happen. Tucker and I spent 8th grade at Prescott Mile High Middle School, which was a real adjustment. Hell, they got more kids in one classroom than we had in our entire school at Skull Valley! And most of the kids are smarter than me, which is to be expected. But nobody makes much fun of me, because Tucker is all the time spreading it around that I'm in tight with the Hells Angels. He loves to tell the story about me beaning one of them, and I just let him go, knowing the actual truth.

It took nearly six months for my broken arm to knit, and I came to hate that cast like nothing else. When it finally came off, I took a hammer to it and busted it into little pieces. It didn't feel as good as I figured it might, but I still enjoyed it some. After a month or so, I noticed my arm didn't feel the same way it had before. The doctor told me it was to be expected with such a serious fracture, and I would just have to deal with it. The problem was, I couldn't seem to pitch over the top like I used to. Even though my right arm is coming along real well, I was still feeling the loss when good old Tucker came to the rescue again.

He said I should try throwing sidearm with my left. And that's what I did, and found it worked alright. Right now, I can manage a decent slider on both sides of the plate, and I'm going to build up strength until I can get a fastball. No matter what the doctor says, I'm fixing to get that arm back to normal so I can throw overhand again, as well.

I have to work hard though. It's already near the end of summer and we're going to Prescott High School come fall. Tucker and I have it set in our minds to both get on the freshman baseball team which starts practice after the turn of the year. That only gives me four or five months to get up to speed, and I'll need every minute of it.

Tucker knows how pressing the time is because at this very moment he's hollering in my ear it's time to practice. So I'll sign off and promise not to lose this book again, and do my best to write in it when I get the chance. I know it's important to document my rise to fame and fortune, so that people behind me will know just how it's done.

Chapter 4

GIL AND TUCKER WALKED DOWN one of the many halls of
Prescott High School. This first year here it seemed they
were perpetually lost, searching for where they were
supposed to be. Sometimes by design. They no longer
looked like twins. The growth spurt Gil had been hoping
for was in full-swing and he now stood 5'6" and had put on
a decent amount of weight. His hands also stretched out,
creating unusually long fingers. Tucker was a good inch
and a half shorter, and stockier, with thick legs and torso.

"I'll never make it four years," said Gil.

"Sure you will," said Tucker. "You ain't gonna leave me
here alone."

Gil sighed. "I'll be lucky if I pass any of my classes this
term."

"You better. Or they won't let you play baseball in the
spring."

"They still might not. How was I to know about
summer baseball camp? And I never did any Little League
or nothing."

"They can't keep you out for that."

"Maybe not. But they'll be favoring the kids that have that kind of experience."

Tucker grabbed him and spun him around. "Knock it off! You're the G-Man, and you're gonna make believers out of them. Understood?"

Gil nodded, then grinned. "Thanks Tuckeroo."

"Come on. Bell's already rung."

They dashed through the hall and eventually found their next classroom. It was the day before Christmas break so the math teacher cut them a little slack for being late, as there wasn't much learning possible on such an eventful day.

When the final bell rang, the halls quickly filled with excited chatter and bustling, all the kids doing their best to escape the prison they'd been locked up in for over three months. Gil and Tucker made their way through the mob, acknowledging some of the friends they'd made their first year.

On the way out the front door, Tucker spied a girl with strawberry-blonde hair, draped low, hiding her dainty facial features. Her head was down, as if studying her feet as she walked alone. Gil saw his friend gazing at her.

"Why don't you say hello this time? It'd be the neighborly thing, seeing as she lives in the apartment below us."

"I know damn well where she lives!" cried Tucker turning his head sharply away from the girl.

Gil shook his head with a grin, then veered from their path and headed toward the object of Tucker's adoration. Tucker tried to grab him, but Gil shook him off.

"Hi," said Gil.

The girl peeked up through the strands of hair. "Hi."

"My friend and I are your upstairs neighbors."

"I've noticed."

"Have you now! Well, My name is Gil and this coward over here is Tucker."

Tucker punched him hard in the arm, and both boys swore they heard a titter from the girl, but they couldn't be positive, since they couldn't see her mouth moving.

"My name's Mandy."

"Lovely name," said Gil. "Tucker here says it would be best if we walk you home. For safety reasons."

Mandy shrugged, then nodded ever so slightly. As the three started off, she mumbled very quietly, "Home's no safer than here."

"What's that?" asked Tucker.

"Nothing," whispered Mandy.

They walked past the buses, all lined up in a row, then turned and headed down the hill. The eight-unit apartment building they lived in was only a few blocks away. They were silent until they started crossing over the playing fields.

Gil said, "Tucker and I are baseball players."

"I've noticed. I watch you practice outside my bedroom window."

"Why didn't you ever come out to the field?"

She wouldn't answer. Gil looked to Tucker and shrugged. "Do you like high school?"

Mandy nodded. "I like anything that gets me out of the house."

"Well, when Tuckeroo and I get on the freshman baseball team, you'll have to come and watch our games."

She looked up at them, the shiny hair falling back, revealing soft green eyes that flitted like they were afraid of being seen. "I'd like that."

"Well, we'd like that, too! Especially Tucker, right buddy?"

Tucker clenched his fists, gritted his teeth and squeezed out, "Sure."

Gil snorted. "See that! He can barely contain his excitement!"

This time they both definitely heard a little giggle come from behind those lovely locks. And they smiled, knowing they had succeeded at their task.

Not another word was said during the rest of the walk, but the three were comfortable together. When they reached the apartments, Mandy's eyes scanned the parking lot. Her body stiffening as she caught sight of a brown sedan.

"Thank you Gil, Tucker. I have to go!"

She dashed the last few yards and slipped through the door of her apartment, not waiting for a goodbye.

"Well, aren't you two the pair!" exclaimed Gil. "Both skittish as a couple of mule deer."

Tucker head-slapped him, and side by side, they climbed the cement steps. Tucker said, "Tomorrow we got to buy a Christmas gift for Al. Something real nice."

"Yeah. Been thinking about it, but can't set my sights on anything. Any ideas?"

"It just has to be something that lets her know how much we feel about her."

Christmas morning, Tucker and Gil were up early, working on the day's big meal. Gil thought it pointless to get a big turkey for just the three of them, so he went for roasted chicken, one of his specialties. It came with all the fixings, and Tucker was kept busy prepping. Alice slept in late. She worked the night before and was scheduled for the evening shift again. Restaurant workers didn't get the holidays off, because everybody else was celebrating and wanted to go out to eat. So, Gil had timed his meal accordingly, making sure she would be well-fed by the time she had to leave.

The food was excellent, and the three consumed nearly enough for five. Afterward, they chatted awhile and then it was down to the presents. They didn't have a tree, because there was no place to put one, and no money for decorations. So when the time came, the boys retrieved a small package from their bedroom and presented it to Alice. She oohed and aahed, not yet even knowing what was inside.

The boys were nervous as she carefully unwrapped it. They had taken two whole days picking it out, and at the time were quite pleased. But now seeing how small it was, they had lumps in their throats.

Alice gingerly placed the wrapping on the sofa and lifted the lid off the small white box. She stared inside for what seemed like forever. Tucker looked nervously at Gil.

"We hope you like it," said Gil.

She pulled out a thin silver necklace with a heart-shaped locket. Etched into the face were two interlocking hearts.

"It opens up," said Tucker nervously.

She unsnapped the locket and stared at a tiny picture of the two boys, head to head, smiling back. She started to cry. Gil and Tucker panicked. They flopped down on either side of her and held her shoulders.

"Sorry, mom," said Gil. "It's all we could afford."

She looked from one to the other. "It's the nicest present anyone's ever given me. With the exception of you two."

More tears followed, on everybody's part. After they had wiped their noses and dried their eyes, Gil placed the necklace around her neck, and Tucker fastened it.

She looked at them with a sly grin, then dashed into her bedroom. She returned with two boxes, a little larger than shoeboxes. She handed them over and Tucker and Gil both wished she hadn't spent her hard-earned money on them.

"Well don't just sit there gawking!" cried Alice, clapping her hands.

Tucker was the first to get his open and his mouth dropped, like in some cartoon. It was a catcher's mitt. A genuine Rawlings. He held it up like the Holy Grail. Gil beamed. Tucker couldn't stop looking from the mitt to Alice. Finally he jumped up and just about knocked her over with a running bear hug.

"Come on, Gil. Show us yours!" he cried.

Gil flipped over the lid on his box, and froze. He had never seen anything so beautiful. A six-fingered glove. With shaking hands he held it up and did one of those cartoon jaw drops like Tucker had.

He stuttered, "Where did you—"

"Japan, believe it or not," said Alice. "And don't look so shocked. You're not the only one who can do research. I found the address of Pat Venditte's father, and wrote him a letter. He was very nice and wrote back telling where I could get one like he got for his son. After all, if you're going to be the next switch-pitcher, you damn well need an interchangeable mitt. Now don't you?"

Gil gazed at it. He placed it on his right hand, then switched to his left.

"Does it fit alright?" asked Alice.

"Like a glove should," said Gil, voice shaking. "I'm going to make you proud mom."

"You always make me proud, Gil. You both do."

The three hugged and laughed and bounced around the living room. All agreed it was the best Christmas ever.

Six weeks later, on a bright, brisk Saturday, Gil and Tucker showed up for freshman tryouts. They arrived two hours early, so they could warm up. They had emptied their savings to purchase cleats. They already had decent pants, jerseys, and caps. And of course they brought their beloved gloves. Tucker also had his catcher's mask.

There was no snow so the tryouts were held outside. An hour after they arrived, other boys began to show. A few were players from the games in the vacant lot, but most were strangers. Many seemed to view Gil and Tucker's presence as an oddity.

When the coach and his assistant arrived, they greeted many of the boys with familiarity. The assistant spotted Gil and Tucker and jogged over to right field where they were playing catch.

"Hey there boys," said the assistant.

"Howdy," said Gil. Tucker just nodded.

"I don't recognize you from summer baseball camp."

Gil said, "Well, that's because we didn't know about it, so we weren't there. We used to live in Skull Valley. Just moved to Prescott."

"Uh-huh. Well, you see, most of the team is already picked at camp. I'm not sure if there are any available spots."

"As long as there are two, that's all you'll need," said Gil with an engaging smile. "Just go and see what the coach has to say."

The assistant frowned, then jogged back to the coach. Gil watched them as they conversed, then swallowed hard when he saw Coach Denning coming their way.

"Let me do the talking," said Gil.

"Don't I always?" said Tucker.

The coach stepped up. "Boys, I'm Coach Denning, and I understand you weren't aware of our system. I know you think this is tryouts, but really it's more of a team meeting. I've already made the cuts for this season."

"That would be a real big mistake, sir," said Gil. "My name is Gil Hayes, and I'm one of the best pitchers you'll ever see, and this here is Tucker, he's my catcher."

Denning grinned a little. "You come with a personal catcher, huh?"

"Yessir," said Gil. "We've been playing together since no higher than your kneecap. And I figure every coach has it in mind to put together a winning team. So it would be a real error on your part to overlook the talent that's in front of you."

Denning's brow wrinkled. "You're pretty confident, aren't you?"

Gil looked at him strangely. "Everybody knows a pitcher without confidence might as well stay on the bench. It's really the only thing he's got going for him."

Coach Denning opened his mouth, but couldn't find any words to counter. He eyed the boys from head to toe, while his mind tried to work out a solution.

Impatiently, Gil said, "You got nothing to lose to let us try out. If we can't cut the mustard, we'll take the axe."

Denning involuntarily chuckled. "Alright, alright! You've convinced me. Go take a seat with the other boys."

Gil and Tucker didn't just jog, they shot off in a dead sprint for the bleachers. Coach Denning couldn't have been more impressed. Talent is something that can't be taught. But hustle is just a state of mind, overlooked by players blessed with natural gifts.

The day started with a description of what was to come. There would be various drills, and then a short five-inning game. The first drill was hitting. One by one, the boys stepped into the batting cage and swung away with all their might, trying their best to impress. Tucker was next to last. He went before Gil and for some reason couldn't catch up to one single ball out of the ten tossed by the confounded machine. He cursed under his breath and walked to the bleachers. Gil slapped him on the back, like he'd clobbered the ball ten times straight.

Gil lined up from the right side. The first ball shot from the mouth of the machine, and he tapped it perfectly to the left. Several players laughed. Denning held up his hand and the assistant paused the machine.

"That's fine, Gil. But let's see you swing away at one."

"Won't do any good, sir," said Gil. "I've tried all my life, but I just don't have the bat speed. But you'll never see a better bunter, and I figure that's exactly what a pitcher needs to be. Turn that thing on again, and I'll show you."

Denning started to argue, but instead waved to the assistant. Gil called out, "To the right it goes, dribbler down the line." The ball sped toward him, and Gil made good his promise. Before the next ball, he called, "Pitcher can't field his position, so right back at him." Sure enough, the bunted ball rolled halfway to the mound and died.

"Fire off another one," said Gil. "But turn that thing up a little. Seems kind of logy."

Denning shrugged, and the assistant made the adjustment.

Gill cried, "Drag bunt." A fastball zoomed toward home plate, and he started to run before it reached him, dragging the bat behind and tapping the ball at the last second. He sped off a few yards then jogged back to the plate. "I'd a made first no sweat."

He called the remainder of his pitches, and they all went where he said they would. He dropped his bat and said, "Was I lying, or no? Best bunter my age you ever saw."

Denning scratched his head as Gil walked by. Young bunters often point their toes toward the mound and square up, which puts them in a bad position to run. This kid kept his feet pointed toward his destination, with his bat held out across the plate, like a seasoned bunter. There was no denying, he was the best he'd seen. But who was he?

The next drill was the 60-yard dash. Gil was all geared up and asked to go first. Denning waved him to the line. He positioned himself, bending his knees, head straight to the path, but cocked down. The explosion had to come in that first step. The starter gun fired, and he leapt forward, arms pumping in sync with his legs, body tight, no flailing. He crossed the finish line still running hard like he had another fifty yards to go.

By the time he turned and jogged back, the assistant was huddled with Denning. "Stopwatch doesn't lie," said the assistant.

Gil jogged up, dying to know his time. Denning shot out a hand and it landed on Gil's chest, stopping him. "You always run a 7 flat?"

"Is that all it was? Shoot. I had it down to 6.8. I swear I did. Let me try again!"

Denning and the assistant stared at him for several moments. Then Denning waved him to the bleachers. He turned to the assistant. "Fastest one in this bunch and JV. Only a couple guys faster in varsity. And yet he claims he's a pitcher."

The assistant shrugged. "We'll see."

The rest of the boys ran out their sprints. Tucker was last and he never was fast, not by a long shot. But, nonetheless, Gil congratulated him on his blazing speed.

When the fielding drills began, Gil approached Denning and said, "Coach, I can catch and toss the ball as good as anyone, but I'd never make it as a position player. My whole life I've trained this body to pitch, like a fine-tuned machine. So if it's okay with you, I'd like to show you my stuff rather than waste your time."

Denning scrunched his eyes, not sure what to make of this kid. But he could see arguing with him would get him nowhere. And it would be easier to cut him if his pitching didn't hold up. He nodded and Gil sat out the drills.

When they were over, the assistant gave the other boys a break while the pitching tryouts proceeded. Gil watched as two other pitchers showed their skills. He noticed they mostly tried to throw fastballs, and that was okay. But when he stepped up to the mound, he asked, "Coach, I get fifteen pitches, right? You mind if I switch them up?"

Misunderstanding what he was asking, Denning said, "Sure. You go ahead and use all the pitches you feel comfortable with."

"Thanks, Coach. And you mind if I use my catcher rather than your guy?"

Denning sighed heavily with exasperation and Gil hurriedly added, "I just figured you'd want to see how well we work together. We have sort of a mental connection."

Denning flipped a hand at him, and Gil excitedly waved in Tucker. Gil leaned in, ball in his right hand. Tucker dropped a sign. Gil went into his signature abbreviated wind-up and hurled. It was a sweet slider to the right and Denning raised an eyebrow.

For the next seven pitches, Gil and Tucker proceeded through Gil's right hand repertoire—four-finger fastball, curveball, splitter. Denning was becoming more impressed. On the ninth pitch, Gil casually moved his mitt to his right hand.

Denning barked, "What are you doing?"

Gil held up his mitt. "It's got six fingers, Coach. It'll be alright."

Denning had been too concentrated to notice the mitt before, but now he studied it. His eyes rose to meet Gil's. "You throw from both sides?"

"You betcha! I'm going to be a famous switch-pitcher. Let me just throw these last balls, you'll see."

Denning stepped to the edge of the mound, arms folded, brain racing. Tucker dropped a sign, and Gil flung the ball. It was a nasty sinker, and a clear strike.

Denning was now completely rapt. Tucker tossed the ball back to the mound. Gil leaned back, formed his grip and shot out a curveball, breaking a good seven inches straight down. Denning whistled softly, then watched quietly as Gil ran through his remaining pitches, some with sidearm, others overhand.

When the drills were over, the assistant divided the boys into two teams and the short game began. Gil didn't get the mound until the last inning. All three batters were righties and Gil threw exclusively from the left. Two of them struck out. The last hit a lazy infield pop-up.

On the way home, Gil and Tucker were silent. Coach Denning had made no hints, and neither knew what the outcome would be. It was a long rest of the weekend.

Monday, after the last bell had rung, Gil sprinted for the bulletin board where the results were to be posted. He ran a finger down the list, his heart beating faster as he didn't see his name. Finally, the last one was him. He breathed out the tension, but it was quickly replaced by dread. Tucker's name was nowhere to be found.

Chapter 5

TUCKER CAREENED AROUND THE CORNER at the end of the hall. He slid to a stop as he saw Gil. They weren't brothers for nothing, and he could tell right away there was bad news coming.

He flung up his hands in disgust. "Are you telling me them damn fools are stupid enough to keep you off their team?!" He stomped toward Gil, shaking his head violently. "Well, that's the most idiotic thing I ever heard of!"

Mandy appeared, out of breath. She instinctively knew better than to approach, silently taking in the situation as it unfolded.

Tucker laid an arm on Gil's shoulder. "Can't blame yourself for what morons do."

"You don't understand!" shouted Gil, pushing the arm away. "I'm on the team."

Tucker's eyes popped. "Well, hot damn!" he looked to Mandy. "G-Man is on the team!" Mandy grinned nervously, sensing there was more. Tucker's smile threatened to burst his face wide open. "So what in the heck's wrong with you?"

"You didn't make the cut, Tucker." Gil's head drooped, unable to look at his friend.

"Shoot, I didn't expect to. They already got two catchers, and both can hit. But at least the coach can recognize talent when he sees it! Congratulations, buddy! You are officially on your way!"

Gil could still not look at him. "It's not the way it was supposed to be."

"What? You think we were going all the way to the majors together? It don't work that way, Gil. You of all people know how few get in the show. You've got what it takes, and you know damn well I never did. So don't be acting dumb."

"I can't do this without you."

Tucker's face hardened. "The hell you can't! You will do this! For me and for Al, or so help me—" His whole body shook with frustration, but the utter grief on Gil's face brought him to his senses. He unclenched his fists and clutched his friend's shoulders.

"You have to understand. There are only a few people like you. And people like me, well, they need people like you to get what they could never even dare dream of. The way I figure, that's what heroes are made for."

Gil looked at him, bleary-eyed. "But you're my catcher."

"That's right. Still am. Who's going to warm up in-between games? And who's going to help you practice new pitches, and keep you in shape in the off-season? And I expect someday, when you're in the majors, you'll suddenly realize that killer sinker of yours just isn't sinking anymore. Or maybe your curve is hanging. Who you gonna call? Me naturally. Now you listen. I will forever be your catcher, Gil. Besides, Al spent good money on my new mitt, and by God it's going to get some use or she'd kill me."

They held each other's eyes until neither could hold back the chuckles. Mandy moved a little closer. Gil said, "We should tell Al before she goes to work."

"I'll take care of that," said Tucker. "Maybe you didn't notice, but says here there's a team meeting going on in the gym, and from what I can see, you're already late."

Gil blanched. "I gotta go!"

"So go!"

Gil waved and shot off down the hall. Mandy stepped up and stood before Tucker. She smiled, and he smiled back. Then she slipped her hand into his and they turned, walking slowly down the hall.

It wasn't long before Coach Denning—a former college and minor league pitcher— became a true believer. Now part of a real team, Gil's abilities blossomed, and he got better with every game. In the beginning of the season, Denning tried persuading Gil to concentrate on pitching with one arm, saying it would be easier to break into the big leagues. Gil wouldn't listen, and after he kept dominating games, Denning quit arguing.

A couple of the opposing teams' coaches complained about the legitimacy of switch-pitching, but Gil set them straight by reciting the newly instituted Venditte Rule which legitimized the practice in the Official Baseball Rules for the MLB. "OBR Rule 8.01 (f). Look it up if you don't believe me," he would say, putting an end to any complaining. If it was good enough for MLB, it was good enough for the naysayers.

In consequence of his sterling debut season with the Prescott Badgers, Gil became a celebrity of sorts. Naturally, some of the varsity players wrote him off as a freak, but it didn't deter him. He was more determined than ever to follow his unlikely path.

During the summer, Gil continued to build up his muscles, and he and Tucker honed his pitches. Tucker also spent plenty of time with Mandy. They'd say they were going fishing, but Gil figured they were doing more than just casting lines. But it was none of his business, and he was happy for them. Mandy started to talk more, and Tucker convinced her to pull her hair back to show her smile, which was a pretty one and worth showing. Yet, Gil always sensed there was something bothering her, but he couldn't place it until one day after the start of their sophomore year.

Mandy came to school and her hair was hanging down over her face, the way it used to be. Well, Tucker had a peek under it and saw a big bruise on her cheek. He asked what it was from, but she wouldn't say. That night, about an hour after the boys had turned in, Gil was suddenly wakened by Tucker shaking him hard.

"Listen," said Tucker.

Gil heard a man yelling and stomping around the apartment below. A woman screamed, followed by another—this one from Mandy. Gil jumped out of bed. There was no need for talking. On the way out of the bedroom, each grabbed a bat. Alice was working late, so there was no need telling her what they were about to do.

As they reached Mandy's door, she came tearing out, a big red splotch spreading on her face, tears pouring. Gil had never seen Tucker so mad. He barreled inside like a charging bull. Mandy's mom was huddled in a corner, covering her face. A man was standing over her screaming. He was a big guy, and Tucker was shorter, but he'd put on weight over the summer and it was all muscle.

The man spun around and it was clear he'd been drinking, a lot. Tucker didn't wait for any explanation. He cocked that bat and swung for the bleachers. The man threw up an arm, trying to block it, but Tucker made a mid-swing adjustment and went under. It was an aluminum bat and it made a harsh clang as it connected with the man's ribs. He went down hard, and Tucker closed in to finish the job. Gil grabbed him from behind and wrestled him back, though it took some doing.

By now, the whole apartment complex was astir and the cops were called. They showed up as Gil was pulling Tucker out of the apartment. Moments later, Alice came home to a real mess. It took a couple hours for everything to be sorted out. The man turned out to be a boyfriend of Mandy's mother, and he tried bringing charges against Tucker, but the police had other plans. This guy had caused trouble in the past, and he was taken away—first to the hospital, then to jail. Tucker was given a stern lecture about leaving such things to the police, but in Gil's ears it sounded like they were praising him. When everyone left, Gil told Tucker it was the best swing he'd ever seen him make. Tucker agreed.

After that night, Tucker stuck to Mandy like glue. He was to be her hero, and he took it quite seriously. Even though the man was ordered not to come near the apartment again, every night, Tucker patrolled the front door with a bat. He and Gil still got their practice in, but something had changed forever. It didn't bother Gil so much. He could see Mandy and Tucker were made for each other, and he had no doubt they would end up hitched. He, however, couldn't be bothered with girls— though a lot had eyes for him. He knew the worst thing a ballplayer can do is find some sort of distraction to take his mind from the game.

Come spring, he easily made the JV team, and Coach Denning was still boss. He told Gil if he kept up his training he could be a star on the varsity team. The season was over before Gil knew it and by now he was standing 5'8" and hoping for a lot more. His body was muscular, especially his legs. His long fingers were strong, but his arms were shorter than he wanted and he hoped the growth spurt would never stop.

Unfortunately, it did. By the start of his junior year, he was 5'10" and going no taller. It was a real blow to him. But he did some research and discovered baseball history was full of players that didn't fit the ideal mold. It shouldn't matter one bit, he told himself. And he determined from then on out, it wouldn't. He knew the most important thing was heart, and he had plenty of that. Enough for a whole team.

To punctuate what he was feeling, he came up with a motto that lasted his whole life, even during the tough times he would encounter ahead—and there would be plenty. He wrote it out in big block letters on a piece of poster board and hung it over his bed: IT'S NOT WHAT THEY SAY. IT'S HOW YOU PLAY.

Trouble began mid-term of that fall. Denning told him if he didn't get his grades up, he wouldn't be eligible to play. This scared a lot of people, no more so than Gil. For the first time in his life, he asked for help. Surprisingly, it was his teachers who came to the rescue. One of the classes he was struggling in was history. They were currently studying the two World Wars, and Gil personally couldn't be bothered why folks chose to kill each other in such a grand fashion.

To spark interest, his teacher created a special assignment for him. He was to report on how the wars affected the major leagues. At first, he was skeptical. But after learning how many great players signed up to fight, leaving the league sparsely populated, it intrigued him. As he dug deeper and saw how the teams dealt with the lack of talent, he became fascinated. By the time it came to give his report, he was an expert. He received an A minus, and a round of applause from his classmates. It was an achievement he never thought he'd care about. But it sure felt wonderful.

English was another stickler. He and his teacher just didn't see eye to eye on how people should talk. Gil often felt bad for her, because she was so determined to help each and every one of her students. But he knew he was a lost cause. Denning interceded, and he and the teacher put their heads together and came up with another special project. This time, Gil was to read a collection of short stories written by some of the great baseball writers of their day.

The book contained twenty-five stories and Gil thought he'd never be able to get through one of them. But as soon as he started, he was hooked. He'd never known how long people had been passionate over baseball. The writers were world-famous: Zane Grey, James Thurber, Mark Twain, Damon Runyon. But to Gil, it seemed as if they all held baseball in higher esteem than themselves, like it was bigger than all of them put together. As he devoured each story, he came to see that he, too, was part of something larger than life. He felt proud and humbled at the same time.

His oral report was scheduled to run twenty minutes, but when he was finished, he had used up the entire class time. He looked up from his notes, and all eyes were waiting for more. He felt nervous, not sure where he'd gone wrong. Then the teacher slowly walked to him, tears in her eyes. She stood before him and said his presentation was eloquent. Gil wasn't sure what the word meant at the time, but he started wondering if finally he was growing some smarts.

The notion was short-lived. About this time, his science teacher jumped on the bandwagon and gave him an assignment which might save his sagging grade. He presented him with a book, not terribly thick, entitled, The Physics of Baseball, written by Robert K. Adair, Ph.D. In the front, it said he was a Sterling Professor Emeritus of Physics at Yale University and a member of the National Academy of Sciences. The lofty title didn't scare Gil any. This was a book on baseball, and he figured he knew everything there was to know. On top of it, he was still feeling pretty high over his successes in English and History.

He dove eagerly into the text and quickly came to a screeching halt when five pages in he realized he hadn't understood a single sentence. Even most of the words were unrecognizable. Such things as drag coefficient, Magnus Force, asymmetric placement, spin axis, among other brain twisters. He had to check the title again to make sure it was indeed about the game he'd grown up living and breathing. It was, and that made it all the more terrible.

The next day, he confronted his teacher with his predicament. The teacher just sat, nodding his head, not even trying to hide a little grin. When Gil was finished, he said, "You'll get it eventually. Just read it through once and don't try and figure everything out. Let it wash over you, and what sticks, sticks. Then go back and read it again. And again, if need be. You want to pass this class, that's the assignment."

Gil fumed. He felt like stuffing that book past that silly grin and down his throat. But not being a violent person by nature, he just dropped the book on the desk and said, "Then I guess I'll fail this class."

"Then you won't pitch."

"You don't understand! I could read this thing fifty times and not get it!"

The teacher sighed. "You underestimate yourself, Gil. And it's my job to prove you wrong. Now I've seen you pitch, and I believe you know more about what this man is talking about than most people on the planet. He's just using different words to describe what you know in your heart."

"Well why doesn't he use regular words then?!"

The teacher ignored the outburst. "Your job is to find three things in there you can prove to me you understand. Next term, you show me three more. Since you'll be in my class your senior year, you can just keep going until you understand it all."

He held out the book like a challenge. Gil glared at it, snatched it up and stomped out of the room. He had never felt so dumb in his life. But he didn't like being bested by anything. The next few weeks, that poor book took quite a beating—mostly from Gil hurling it against his bedroom wall. One night, however, he woke from a dead sleep, his brain humming.

He grabbed the text and turned to the section he'd been reading. The writer was discussing the effect of the stitches on a ball's path, namely, how different placements of the stitches as they pass through air cause varying resistances, thereby, varying the paths. Gil realized he had always known that was true. He'd just known it in a different way, using different words.

His eyes glinted as he reread the section. He turned to the next and continued reading. Lucky it was a Friday night, because he was up awful late.

When it was time for his report, he told the teacher he needed the entire class to meet in the gymnasium, where he would give his demonstration. Tucker was allowed to leave his class to help. Gil proceeded to walk his peers through the intricacies of air resistance as they related to the throwing of a baseball. To make his point, he threw several pitches to Tucker, showing them how different pitches react differently, and why.

He had only scratched the surface of what the man was writing about in his book, but when he was finished, his classmates and teacher were highly impressed. So much so, the teacher told him he could keep the book over Christmas break, so he'd have a head start on the next term. This time, Gil thanked him repeatedly. He had a hunch if he could crack the code and unlock the secrets in that little book, it would make him one of the most feared pitchers in the game.

Chapter 6

"YOU SEE THIS LITTLE BOOK HERE?" began Gil, holding it out so his classmates could get a look. "It took me one whole year to get through." There were a few titters, but he ignored them, confident in where he was going.

"And the only way I got through it was I finally came to understand the man who wrote it was using a foreign language. At first, I was upset because baseball is something I know in my own language. What was he doing using words I couldn't understand? I wrestled with this for a very long time until I saw the light. I realized there are different ways of looking at the truth. I had one way, and he had another. Both equally valid. Kind of like looking through a window with one eye or the other. You see the same thing, just from a different angle."

Gil shuffled his notes and cleared his throat. His classmates didn't dare interrupt, because they could see he was speaking from the heart, and were intrigued as to what mystery he had uncovered.

"As I began to understand this man's language, I realized if I managed to grasp how he was looking at the truth, and combine it with how I saw it, I'd be able to look deeper at what I have chosen to do in my life. The picture would flush out, revealing things my way of looking couldn't do alone.

"It was the most difficult thing I have ever done. Mostly because in the beginning I was stubborn. I didn't want to accept there was any other way to see what I thought I already knew. But I was wrong, and after I accepted that, I forced myself to see my game through the eyes of someone who saw it differently.

"Well, I thought I was on a roll. I had figured out much of the language, and yet, partway through, I became afraid. I got scared if I went any further, the way I saw the game would be ruined. All this analyzing and theorizing might take away the magic. But, once again, I was wrong. I kept on reading and on a day I'll never forget, I realized the opposite had occurred. All the science involved had come to make the game even more beautiful. Because I saw nature had a hand in it all. And when you get down to it, that's what physics is, just nature. It's the way the world works."

Gil looked to the back of the room and saw his teacher, leaning back, hands clasped behind his head, that same grin on his face. This time, Gil grinned back.

"But let me get to the real point. About the tenth time I read this book, I wondered if I was missing a beat. Sure, I understood what this man was talking about, mostly. But how could it help me? Now, maybe some of you saw me pitch last year."

It was an understatement to be sure. Due to injuries on the varsity team, two of the JV pitchers were sent to play with the seniors, and Gil had moved up in the rotation, becoming the ace of the JV team. He pitched masterfully, and was instrumental in leading his team to the conference championship at their level. They won, due to a shutout he pitched. All the students in the class remembered, and cheered for him until the teacher told them to pipe down.

"I appreciate that," said Gil in acknowledgement. "I was proud of how I pitched, but since then I've learned how to put this man's lessons to use. Since physics is all about probabilities, a person can narrow down what is likely to work and what is not. So, I filtered through all the learning and asked myself, what can I take from this that will help me be better? And by that I mean only one thing, getting more people out at the plate. So for the rest of my talk, I'm going to show you why, come this spring, the other teams better watch out, friends. Because I've got a secret weapon, and it's this little book."

"G-Man, G-Man, G-Man!" chanted the class. For five minutes they wouldn't shut up until Gil took control. Then he methodically proceeded to regale his classmates with the science of pitching.

It was the bottom of the ninth, and Gil jogged back to the dugout, his teammates cheering him in. The team was down two runs to the Mojave Rattlers, but he had given them hope. And baseball is a game built around hope, right up to the last out. His sacrifice bunt had put the catcher on second, in scoring position. Gil, not having pitched that day, had pinch-hit for the pitcher.

As he waded through his jubilant teammates slapping him on the back, he ignored his coach's outstretched hand. He and Coach Reynolds were not friends. And Gil had never seen the point in being friendly with someone he wasn't friends with.

He saw Chip Benson, head in his hands, and plopped down next to him.

"Nice bunt, Gil," said Chip.

"Trying my best to get you up," said Gil.

Chip was, until recently, the best hitter. But he had fallen on hard times and hadn't had a knock in the last two games. He was 0-3 in this outing, as well.

"That might not be such a good idea," muttered Chip.

A crack of the bat lifted their eyes to the field in time to see the leadoff man make first, moving the catcher to third. Chip quietly groaned.

"Everybody gets in a slump," said Gil.

Chip shook his head. "I can't afford one, not today. You know who's in the stands."

Every member of the team knew. The Prescott Badgers were always a powerhouse, and thus attracted many scouts. This game, late in a tightly contested season, however, had proved to be a real attraction, and there were at least four scouts present that they knew of. For some of the players, it was a do or die situation. Their baseball careers could go on from here, or fade forever.

"I just can't figure out what I'm doing wrong," mumbled Chip.

"You're aiming," said Gil. "Been meaning to tell you that."

A spark of hope came to Chip's eyes. "Come on, Gil. You can't just leave it at that."

"Coach says he doesn't like me going over his head, giving advice."

"Screw the coach! Hell he hasn't even let you switch-pitch all season. If he had, we would've already wrapped the conference up by now. Besides, you taught Jimmy Reese to throw a slider, and now look at him. He's already got offers from three schools. Just give me a little tip."

Gil saw Coach Reynolds was concentrated on the field, and leaned in. "Here's the deal. A full swing takes about

180 milliseconds from start to finish. A little over the time it takes to blink."

"Strike two!" bellowed the umpire.

"Hurry up, Gil!" said Chip.

"Okay, after you've started your swing you only have about 50 milliseconds to make any adjustments to the ball. After that, the last half moment before the ball crosses the plate, there's nothing you can do about your swing. You've made your decision, and it would take too long for your brain to tell your body to change what it's doing."

"So?"

"So, what I seen you doing is trying to adjust your swing too late. In truth, you could close your eyes once your swing is in gear and have just as good a chance at hitting the ball, maybe better. At that point, you have to feel the hit, Chip. Trust in it. Understand?"

Chip let it sink in, nodding slowly. "I guess I thought I was quick enough to adjust."

"No one's quick enough, Chip. It ain't your fault. It's just physics."

"Strike three!" announced the umpire and the second guy in the lineup trudged back to the dugout.

As the next man strode up to the plate, Coach Reynolds yelled, "Benson, on-deck! Get with the game son!"

Chip started for the steps then turned back to Gil. "Close my eyes, huh?"

"Would I ever steer one of my teammates wrong?"

Chip grinned and climbed out of the dugout. The home crowd hushed as the man at bat faced a 2-2 count. He was not known as a power hitter, but he was fast. And that's exactly what he needed when he landed a slow roller to the left of the shortstop. He beat the throw by half a step and the crowd went crazy.

Chip took one last look to the dugout and saw Gil giving him the thumbs-up. He nodded firmly and walked to the plate with all the swagger he could muster—given there were two outs and bases loaded. The pitcher had faced him on other occasions and, despite the recent slump, was nervous to throw anything good. But he obviously couldn't afford the walk. He tried backing him off the plate with a fastball inside, but Chip spit on it and didn't budge. Ball one. The next toss went wide on purpose, trying to get him to flail, but Chip was busy clearing his mind, waiting for the right pitch. The next one was a curveball, not Chip's specialty, and he let it go for a strike. The count was 2-1.

He snuck a peek at the catcher and could tell he was nervous to let his pitcher go to 3-1. Everything in his experience told him they were coming after him, and he wasn't mistaken. It came fast and high, and he signaled his body to swing. Midway through, it felt good, and he now knew there was nothing more he could do. He closed his eyes, and felt a familiar shudder as the bat connected cleanly.

It was a whistling line drive that didn't stop until smacking into the right field fence, taking a sharp angle away from the right fielder. He took off, lumbering toward first. But there was no need to hurry. The runners had started on contact, and the speed on the bases paid off. It was a bases-clearing double to win the game.

The Badgers swarmed the field, everyone zeroing in on Chip. But he pushed past, seeking out Gil at the back of the pack. He lifted him up, and spun him in the air

"We did it Gil!" he cried.

"You did it, Chip! Now put me down you big ape, you're crushing me to death."

After the excitement faded, Gil grabbed his mitt from the dugout and headed to the parking lot. On the way, he saw Chip and his dad talking to one of the scouts. Gil grinned. He was a deserving player and was happy for him.

Not so much for himself, though. He spotted Tucker and Mandy, standing beside Tucker's truck which he had bought shortly into his senior year. He was working at the garage nearly full-time now and had plenty of money to burn.

"Nice sac, Gil," said Tucker with a grin.

Gil grunted. "Let's get the hell out of here. This is a waste of my time."

Coach Denning saw Gil climbing into the truck and called out. But it was too late. It made him even more irate. He spun, and went in search of Coach Reynolds. He found him finishing up his game notes in the dugout.

"I asked you to let him pitch a full inning," said Denning, barely containing his ire.

"What you asked," said Reynolds, glancing up from his notebook, "is that I let him switch-pitch for an inning."

"I told you I had a scout here. It was Jaggard. He came for Gil."

"Well, he didn't miss much."

"What the hell is your problem?!" roared Denning.

"You are the problem. You let that boy think he has something."

"He does have something. If you'd give him the chance."

Reynolds finally met his eyes. "He's a novelty. It made you look good in JV, nothing else. No place for it in real baseball."

"You mean in your baseball. The majors have already accepted it."

"They deal with it. They've never accepted it and they never will. Once this Venditte washes out, it'll be over. Just a passing thing."

"I disagree."

"And that's why you coach freshman and JV."

Denning felt a distinct urge to pummel the man, but he held back, knowing nothing would get through his inflexible mind. "You don't have the right to hold back a player."

"The hell I don't! I'm the coach, and this is my team. Don't you forget it. But Gil's got no future anyway. Better to have him face reality earlier rather than later. Now get out of my dugout."

Denning started up the steps, but stopped at the last one and turned to Reynolds. "I can't wait to see your face when he proves you wrong."

"You have to calm down, buddy," said Tucker, cruising down Montezuma St.

"And why's that?!" exclaimed Gil. Mandy was sitting between them on the front seat and sank back, out of the firing range.

"Five innings! That's how many I've been allowed to pitch this season. And always in relief. Always with the left hand. You're a reliever, says the High and Mighty Coach Reynolds."

"I know, I know," said Tucker.

"Do you? So how much longer would you say I should wait before I stop being calm? Hey! How about the rest of the season? Then all the open tryouts are over. How about then? Would that be long enough, buddy!"

Tucker didn't have an answer for this, so he kept his mouth shut. When they reached the apartment building,

Gil headed inside. Mandy turned to Tucker who was gripping the steering wheel, staring out at the vacant lot.

"He's going to leave, isn't he?" she asked.

"Uh-huh."

"He won't graduate if he does. Isn't there something you can say?"

Tucker turned to her. "He don't give a rat's ass about graduating, and I can't blame him. He was born to do one thing, Mandy. That's all he's good at. So here's what I have to say. I'll do anything he wants me to do to help him reach his dream."

That night, the two boys made their plans. In two weeks, the Major League Baseball Scouting Bureau was holding a tryout in Phoenix, open to any player 16 years or older. Gil went online and filled out the entry form, the fee to be paid on the day of the tryouts. It happened the Badgers had a game on that day, but this held little concern. Gil knew he wasn't going to pitch, so what was the point?

As the days crept by, the two friends worked feverishly to get Gil ready. Not a word was said to Alice, and though Tucker understood why Gil was staying mum, he felt it was unfair to keep her in the dark. Four days before the tryouts, he said as much to Gil.

"She'll find out soon enough," responded Gil. "After I'm drafted."

"But why not let her know now? She's always supported what you do."

Gil's cheek twitched. "Because on the off chance she says she doesn't want me to leave, I'd have to stay. I'd have no choice. And then I'd resent it, and her."

Tucker digested this. "Then I guess we're on our own. Does the team know?"

"No. They're a good bunch of guys, and I hate to let 'em down, but it's what I gotta do. And I don't want to talk about it anymore. You think you can run me over to the bus station? I need to get my ticket to Phoenix."

Tucker had to work very hard to keep his anger in check. He clenched his jaw and tried to slow his breathing before he responded. Gil took it as hesitation.

"Never mind. I know you're busy. I'll just walk on over."

"You shut the hell up Gil Hayes! Or so help me I'll knock you a good one, and you'll go to that tryout with a shiner! Ain't nobody taking you to Phoenix but me! Understood?"

"Sure, Tuckeroo. Okay, sure."

"And I don't want to hear another word about it!"

"And you won't. I just didn't want you to have to take off work."

Tucker's jaw flapped open in disbelief. He shook his head violently, muttering angrily to himself. Gil quickly tossed an arm over his shoulders and squeezed tight.

"I'm sorry, brother. I wasn't thinking. It's not my specialty as you of all people know. I'd be honored to have you chauffeur me. Might want to bring Mandy along though. After I catch the eye of some scout and he whisks me off to the majors, it won't be much fun for you driving home alone."

Tucker looked at him and smiled. "On the contrary. That'll be the greatest moment of my life."

Chapter 7

As is often the case in life, things didn't go as planned. There were three hundred players at the tryouts. That didn't bother Gil so much as the cattle call process. With little time to shine, it seemed impossible a scout could judge the talent of any one player.

Gil ran the 60-yard dash in 6.9, and it was assumed he was a position player. He informed them he was a pitcher, and after refusing to do anything but bunt during the hitting drill, the initial stir over his speed was quickly forgotten.

It was the pitching tryout, however, that sealed his fate. Each man was permitted ten pitches, and were told to throw only fastballs. It was made crystal clear if they could not throw at least 90 mph, they had little chance of success. Gil voiced his displeasure. He insisted a good pitcher was more than a fastball thrower. His argument fell on deaf ears. On his third pitch, he managed to reach 90, barely, but when he switched his glove to show off his other arm, he was immediately removed from the mound.

All the pent-up frustration over Coach Reynolds finally burst out and he made a scene. It didn't help his cause. It did, however, draw the attention of another young hopeful by the name of Danny Kane. He was tall, well-built, with blonde hair, and handsome in a devilish sort of way. As Gil ranted, Danny egged him on, eager to be part of the spectacle. When the organizers tried escorting Gil off the field, Danny backed him up, trying to pick a fight, and assuring he, too, was out of the running.

After the two were evicted and standing outside the ballpark, Gil continued to fume and stomp about, but Danny acted as if it was all a hoot. He laughed and slapped his sides like it had been the most fun he'd ever had.

"What do you got to be laughing about?" asked Gil angrily. "Why would you do such a damn fool thing, sticking up for me?"

"You're welcome," said Danny with a scampish grin. "Name's Danny Kane. I play second base, shortstop if needed." He held out a hand.

Gil ignored it. "Because of me, you lost your chance as well!"

Danny would not be put off. He shoved his hand forward a little farther. Gil sighed heavily and grasped it firmly.

"Gil Hayes."

Danny smiled. "I like your style, Gil Hayes. Been to a lot of these damn things, and never saw anybody talk back or try and speak their mind."

"Well, hell, I don't know any other way," said Gil, slumping. "That's my problem."

"Teams won't admit it, but they like players with grit. Nothing wrong with being mouthy when you're right."

"Well that's just great, but none of the team reps in there liked it, and I don't know what I'm going to do now."

"Lots of other tryouts in the next few months. All the way into July. I could use a traveling companion."

"What are you talking about?"

"You can't lay down and die first time out. You and me, we'll get where we need to be. If you're good, they'll find you."

"You better believe I'm good!"

"I believe it. Probably better than me. Probably better than a lot of the players that get drafted early on. But it's not only the ones with talent that get to the show. It's the ones that just won't go away, no matter what."

Gil studied this person grinning back at him. He seemed older than he appeared. And he had a manner that implied everything came easy for him. So how did he know about failure? How could he know about such things?

"So you up for a road trip?" asked Danny. "Next stop is Houston. There's an open tryout this Tuesday."

"How would we get there?"

Danny cocked his head toward a classic 1978 Pontiac Firebird Gold Trans Am in mint condition. "It's my old man's baby. He said I could take it for a spin."

Gil had never seen such a fine machine. "Sure would be fun. But I only had enough money for the entrance fee with about three hundred left over."

"Figured you'd get picked up right off, huh?" asked Danny with a sly wink. "Maybe get a big fat signing bonus to boot?"

Gil blushed. "Something like that."

"Well, don't you worry. Dear old daddy is loaded out the yang. And I happen to have a couple of credit cards that'll take care of us just fine."

Gil narrowed his eyes. "Why would you do that for me?"

Danny playfully aped his skeptical look. "I already told you. I like your style. And ballplayers need to stick together. Am I right?"

Before Gil could make sense of all this, Tucker and Mandy came running across the parking lot. They had witnessed the awful scene in the tryouts and were at a loss for words. Gil met Tucker's eyes, made a wry grin and shrugged. Tucker mimicked him.

"Sorry you had to drive all this way for nothing," said Gil.

"At least you put on a good show. They're still talking about it in there."

"Too bad it's not about how great my pitching is."

"They'll be other tryouts."

Danny cut in. "That's what I've been trying to tell him! Next time, he'll knock 'em dead. Won't you Gil?"

Tucker eyeballed Danny, who grinned and held out a hand. "Danny Kane."

Tucker stared at the hand like it was something foreign. Gil jumped in. "This is my best friend, and his gal, Mandy."

Danny kept his hand hanging out in the air, and said, "Pleased to meet you Mandy. You too, Gil's best friend."

Mandy smiled. Tucker shrugged, and shook Danny's hand firmly. "Name's Tucker. Nice of you to stick up for my buddy in there."

"Seemed like the right thing to do."

After that, no one appeared to have anything more to say. Tucker broke the awkward silence with, "If we're to beat the godawful traffic in this city, we better get a move on."

Gil blurted, "I'm going with Danny."

"What's that?"

"He's moving on to more tryouts and offered to take me along. We're not going to stop until we get what we want. Isn't that right, Danny?"

"That's the plan."

"You're talking crazy, Gil," said Tucker with a scowl. "Come on."

"I can't go back, Tucker! How am I supposed to face mom? And what am I going to do back there anyway? I need to move forward."

Gil and Tucker locked eyes. Of all people, Gil needed him to understand. Silently, they conversed. Finally, Tucker nodded.

"But you don't even know this man, Gil!" said Mandy.

"He's a ballplayer. We both want the same thing. And he's got wheels. Feast your eyes." He pointed to the Trans Am.

Tucker, mechanic extraordinaire and classic car aficionado couldn't help but be impressed. "78-79 Limited Edition. You packing the standard 403 cubic inch 185hp, or the Pontiac-built 400 custom option with 220 horsepower?"

"Whatever you say!" laughed Danny. "I only drive it. Have a look under the hood."

"Don't mind if I do. Mandy, go on and help Gil get his stuff out of the truck." He tossed her the keys.

"That's it? But Tucker!"

"Go on. Gil's made up his mind. Just want to make sure this rig is gonna get them where they're going."

Gil slapped him on the back, grabbed Mandy's arm and they hustled across the parking lot to Tucker's truck. Danny walked to his car and popped the hood. Tucker expertly examined the engine.

"Looks like it's never been driven."

"It's my dad's. More of a status symbol than anything."

"That's a shame. Made to run."

Tucker furthered his study, and Danny said, "So Gil's a switch-pitcher, huh?"

"Best you'll ever see."

"No doubt, since I've never seen one." He chuckled at his own joke. Tucker didn't. "Is he really as good as he says?"

Tucker leaned back and went face to face. "Gil don't lie. And neither do I. Now there ain't much I can do to stop him going with you. But I can hunt you down and kill you if anything bad happens to him. You understand?"

Danny recoiled, then gained his normal composure. "Well, I understand Gil's lucky to have a friend like you. That's for sure. And you have nothing to worry about. As I told him, I just need a traveling companion. Trying to get into the big leagues is tough enough without doing it alone."

Tucker appeared satisfied and continued his inspection. "What position you play?"

"Second base. Shortstop in a pinch. You play?"

"I'm Gil's catcher. Always will be. Just not good enough to go where he's going."

"That's too bad."

"Yeah. Otherwise, I'd be going to these tryouts with him, not you."

"Hey, man. You don't have to like me. I'm just trying to help out your friend."

Tucker cocked his head. "And I appreciate that. More than you know. I'm sorry I'm being rough on you. It's just hard to see him go. We've never been apart more than a day or two. You have a cellphone?"

"Who doesn't?"

"Gil. That's who. Says he can't be bothered. Only thing he cares about is baseball. I want you to put my number in your phone. And you call me if he needs anything, and I mean anything. Day or night. You get it?"

"Sure, Tucker," said Danny pulling out his phone. "So you think she'll make it? We have a lot of miles to go."

Tucker pulled back, grinning, and said, "Oh, she'll do just fine. Just make sure you have enough weight in her or she's liable to take off for the moon."

At Tucker's truck, Gil retrieved the small suitcase he had packed in anticipation of being drafted. He smiled wryly to himself at the thought. So naïve. Mandy stood back from the truck, silently fretting. Gil caught sight.

"Don't be looking like that."

"How else should I look? You're leaving us, Gil. What is Tucker going to do?"

"He'll be just fine. And if I stayed in Prescott, he'd learn to hate me because I'd turn into a wreck if I wasn't pitching."

"He could never hate you!"

Gil smiled. "You're right about that. But I'm right on this thing. I have to go. And I need you to do one thing for me. It's very important."

"Anything you want, Gil."

He grabbed her shoulders, looking deep into her eyes. "Be true to him, Mandy. Don't ever break his heart. He's so in love with you, it would kill him. And that'd be like killing half of me."

She slowly shook her head in horror. "I would never—"

"Alright then. And when you two make plans to get hitched, you better let me know. I wouldn't miss that for the world."

Mandy choked up. "You'll be the first to know."

Gil hugged her. "Keep an eye on Al, as well. She's going to be awful sad at first. But you explain to her why I had to do this. Okay?"

She buried her head in his shoulder and nodded. He could hear soft sobbing and he rocked her back and forth.

When they got back to Danny's car, Tucker was in the driver seat revving up the engine. He climbed out as Gil walked up.

"Everything meet with your approval?" asked Gil.

Tucker looked to the car and then to Danny. "They'll do. You best get on the road. Danny says you got some miles ahead of you."

"Let me take that," said Danny, grabbing Gil's suitcase.

As he stowed it in the trunk, Tucker led Gil a few steps away. He pulled out his wallet and took out a sheaf of bills. "I figure you might need this."

Gil waved the money away. "You work hard for that."

"That's right! And it means I get to choose how I use it. Now you take this, and I don't want any arguments. I'm serious, Gil. Don't mess with me. Not now."

Gil nodded, and took the wad. "Thanks, buddy. Will you let Al know I'll be alright."

"I'll tell her. But she'll want to hear it from you."

"I'll call her as soon as we get where we're going."

"You better. You don't want Ice on your bad side."

They both laughed nervously, knowing the time had come. "Well, I'll see you around," said Gil, voice shaking.

"I expect. And Gil, don't ever let anyone make you quit. Never." He slapped Gil on the shoulder and took off at a fast pace, not looking back. Mandy caught up to him and saw giant tears slowly crawling down his stony face. She wrapped an arm around his waist and they walked on.

Danny stepped up to Gil. "You ready man?"

Gil nodded. "Been ready all my life. Let's get this damn show on the road."

Chapter 8

THREE HOURS INTO THE DRIVE, approaching the New Mexico border, Danny shook his head in wonderment. It had only taken a short time for Gil to lay out the entirety of his life. He'd left nothing out, finding it easy to talk to a stranger about his past. Danny had listened quietly up until now.

"You have to be putting me on, man!" he exclaimed. "If it weren't for the Hell's Angels, I'd say you grew up in Mayberry and your name is Opie. I never knew people like you still existed in the modern world. No smartphone, email, Facebook—"

"Never saw the point in any of that stuff."

"There has to be something else you do besides play ball."

"I juggle. I'm up to five balls now. It helps me keep both arms balanced, in sync, so to speak. It's good warm-up for switch-pitching."

"I knew it had to be connected to baseball somehow. Exactly how far have you been away from home?"

Gil looked out at the foreign landscape. "Here."

Danny broke into laughter. "You mean you've never seen an ocean?"

Gil felt his face reddening, and blurted, "If it ain't in Arizona, I ain't seen it! Don't see what difference it makes. Ocean's not such a big deal."

Danny stifled his laughter. "Bigger than anything you've ever seen, except a desert."

Gil shrugged and turned away. Danny realized he'd taken his teasing a little too far. He leaned back, and stretched his fingers around the steering wheel, wondering how to smooth the moment.

"You want a beer?"

Gil shot him a look. "I don't drink."

"Good deal. Then you can drive." He eased the car to the side of the highway.

"You kidding?!"

"Safer that way, especially if I'm drinking," said Danny. After retrieving a small cooler from the trunk, he walked around to the passenger's side. Gil hadn't moved. "You do have a license don't you?"

"Of course! We're not that backwards in Prescott."

"Then get behind the wheel. We're wasting time."

Gil looked up at him. "Only rigs I ever drove was Tucker's truck and my mom's old heap. I've never driven anything this nice."

"It's all the same. Except this is a lot more fun. Besides, it's just highway. Keep going straight until I tell you otherwise. We need to make El Paso by night if we're going to stick to our timetable."

Gil still didn't budge. Danny said, "What is it? Can't you drive a stick?"

Gil whipped open his door. "Of course I can drive a stick! Only way I know how!"

He brushed past Danny, who said, "Now we're talking! Just be easy pulling out in first, she always acts like she's in a drag race." He grabbed a beer from the cooler, and settled in for the ride.

Gil took his position, familiarizing himself with the car. He shifted into first and popped the clutch. The car shot out like a bullet, tearing along the shoulder, spewing out clouds of pulverized sandstone. Without checking his rearview mirror, he swerved onto the highway and upshifted.

Danny howled, slapping his knee and slopping beer on his crotch. After Gil had reached top gear and slowed his heartbeat to an acceptable level, they cruised on down the highway, the powerful engine gurgling happily.

After a few chugs from his can, Danny said, "Well, now I know all about you, I guess it's time for me to spill."

As the miles clicked off, and the beer in the cooler dwindled, Gil was treated to a vision of a world he had never imagined. Danny grew up in Torrey Pines, north of San Diego. His father was a hotshot lawyer, easily covering the half million annual tab required to live in such an exclusive community.

As a child, he attended the elite Del Mar Hills Academy, where he was constantly on the verge of being expelled. As he grew up, his father wanted him to concentrate on golf, which he considered an appropriate sport for his privileged son—not to mention their estate bordered on an exclusive, private course. Danny, however, chose to play baseball, mostly to rile his demanding father. High school was spent getting into as much trouble as possible and playing second base for the mediocre school team.

Upon graduating, he was informed he was to follow in his dad's footsteps by becoming a lawyer, eventually joining the family firm. Danny was resistant. He insisted he be allowed to follow his dream to become a baseball player. As Gil listened, however, he could tell, that this dream was more about driving his father crazy, and less about any real passion for the game.

His father relented—somewhat. He told Danny he would give him one year to reach his goal. After that, he would toe the line, or be cut off from the money. Danny spent the first summer going to tryouts, with no success. In the fall and winter, he partied hard and chased girls, doing his level best to forget about his predestined future.

Early spring, he attended two tryouts in California, with no luck. Now, just turned nineteen, he was on a deadline. As he talked, though, Gil saw no signs of pressure over the dwindling time left to him.

On the outskirts of El Paso, Danny's phone rang. He checked the Caller ID and said, "Leave me alone, old man," and tossed the cell on the dash.

"Your father, huh?" asked Gil. "Probably worried about you."

Danny snorted and crushed his latest can. "Hardly. It's the car he's worried about."

"I thought he said you could take it out for a spin."

"He probably did. But I doubt he thought I'd take it cross country."

"Well, why'd you take it then? You must have a car of your own."

"Of course. It's one of those new Chargers. But it's not as fun as this. Screw him. Thing's not supposed to be sitting in a garage anyway."

They drove on, Gil getting more and more anxious. "He won't call the cops will he?"

Danny guffawed, and slurred, "Not likely. If he does, he knows I'll call him to bail me out, like I always do. No worries, dude. We're all set. And nothing's going to stop our forward progression. Hey! I like that. We are on a forward progression. Nice, huh?"

"I think you're on a bender. I'm stopping at the first motel."

"Motel? Gil, you have to get with the program. We go in style or we don't go at all. Now keep your eyes out for the fanciest hotel in this city."

Gil had never stayed in a hotel—or a motel, for that matter, so he had some time trying to locate one that would satisfy his discerning traveling companion. After much deliberation, they finally settled on the Double Tree Hilton, mostly because of the highly touted rooftop pool. Danny consented because he claimed he was feeling a little hot and sweaty after such a long drive, and needed a nice dip.

When they found the hotel did not have suites, he ordered up two rooms, each with a king bed, giant TV, WiFi, and stocked refrigerator.

Gil thought it was ridiculous to go to the expense of two rooms, but Danny blithely ignored him. After they changed out of their baseball clothes, they went in search of sustenance. There were three on-site restaurants and Danny immediately opted for the most expensive, the Sunset Terrace. The bird's eye view of downtown was glittering and impressive. They could even see the Rio Grande. Danny teased Gil as he pressed his face against the glass of the floor-to-ceiling windows, gawking at the sight.

As they waited for their food, Gil began to feel self-conscious. Everyone else in the restaurant, including Danny, were dressed in fine clothes, while he wore his standard uniform of faded jeans and t-shirt. He felt even more out of place when he noticed two girls—of about the same age spread as he and Danny—seated with their parents at a nearby table. The sisters were not so subtly peering over their parents' shoulders. They were mostly eyeing Danny, who Gil noticed was keenly aware of it, and taking full advantage.

He leaned back in his chair, cocked his square jaw, and idly tossed his blond hair to one side. Then, as if merely an afterthought, his eyes scanned the room with a bored nonchalance. When they landed on the two girls, he made a big deal of feigning surprise at seeing such a glorious site. His eyebrows raised a notch and he focused in. The sisters shrank back under his appraising stare. Ever so slowly, a wide, mischievous grin appeared, then finally the denouement—he winked. The girls swooned. And he turned away, just as the waiter delivered the food. It was a masterful performance, and Gil shook his head and chuckled.

"What's so funny, my man?" asked Danny.

"You, that's what," said Gil smothering a laugh in his linen napkin.

"You like that, huh? It's a talent, I admit. But necessary if you want the bees to come to you."

"You blind? They're with their parents."

Danny's brow puckered. "Is that a problem?"

Gil could barely contain his mirth. "You'll get none of that action tonight."

"You want to bet?"

"I do not! All I want is to fill my belly and get some sleep. Long day tomorrow."

"There are other ways to recharge the batteries."

Just the casual way he said it made Gil crack up. He tried to hold back, but the laugh burst forth, drawing eyes from around the room. Danny acted like nothing had happened, and this hyena across the table was no acquaintance of his. Which made Gil laugh even more. After he finished, the two got down to the serious business of eating. They polished off their food and desserts in record time.

Danny called for the bill, paid with a credit card, and stood up.

He leaned across the table and said conspiratorially, "Tomorrow, my friend, we cross the most miserable, boring desert you'll ever see. It's called Texas, for short. It'll take us all day. Now, the bet is this. If I hook up with one of those girls tonight, you drive—the whole thing. If I don't, I drive. If we both score, we split the task. Deal?"

Gil, feeling naively confident the deed was impossible, smirked. "You're on."

Danny, all business, pushed his chair under the table. He sauntered toward the exit, strategically selecting his path to pass by the girls' table. He made a point not to make eye contact, but instead, cocked his head to Gil and said, "Hey buddy, looks like a great night for a moonlight swim on the roof. What do you say?"

Gil was caught off guard and almost blew his cue, but recovered, saying, "A beautiful night at that, pal. Let's do it."

It must have taken a while for the girls to elude their parents, because they didn't show up on the roof until shortly past ten. Danny and Gil had been there for quite some time, swimming laps and generally goofing around. Gil didn't have a swimsuit, and Danny said he should skinny dip—better to attract the ladies. Gil was not amused and chose to where a pair of old cutoff shorts. After they had been there an hour, he felt sure the girls weren't coming and told Danny they should call it a night.

That's when the sisters showed. Both wore small bikinis, leaving little to the imagination. They were thrilled to find the boys still there and quickly joined them in the pool. The older one, Linda, was soon to be a sophomore in college, and gravitated to Danny, as they were closer in age. While the younger one, Celia, had just graduated high school, and cozied up to Gil.

At first, everything went swimmingly. Danny told the girls he and Gil were soon to be professional baseball players, and this seemed to hold their interest—but only for a short time. At Danny's urging, Gil retrieved his juggling balls from his room. He entertained for several minutes, but it appeared as if the girls had other things on their minds. An unspoken communication occurred between them and Linda announced she and Danny were going to explore the hotel. Danny winked at Gil as they departed, arm in arm.

Not wasting anymore time, Celia said to Gil, "Let's go back to your room."

"Um. Sure. It's got a big TV."

"Well, yeah! Duh. Come on."

She grabbed Gil's arm and they moved swiftly into the hotel. In Gil's room, she plopped down on the bed and laid back.

"Do you have any pot?"

"Wh—what?!"

"P-O-T. Do you have any?"

"No! Besides, they don't allow smoking in the rooms."

"Whatever. How about booze?"

"I don't drink."

She looked at him in disbelief. "How boring is that. So what do you do?"

"I told you. I'm a pitcher. Switch-pitcher to be exact."

She rolled her eyes. "Please! I've had enough baseball for one evening!"

He stood near the bed, remaining water droplets from the pool mixing with beads of cold sweat. He had absolutely no idea how to proceed. Nor did he really care to go any further with this. It's not that he didn't like girls and sometimes fantasize over them, but to this point in his life, he had found them merely a distraction. He did not, however, want to insult this girl, or make her think she wasn't attractive. He inched toward the bed and finally found the right moment to ease down next to her outstretched legs.

There was no outcry or protest so he swallowed hard and inched a hand closer to the closest leg. Ever so slowly, he lifted his hand and laid it on top.

"Ew! Your hands are clammy!" cried Celia.

Gil leapt from the bed, frantically wiping his hands on his damp shorts. Celia got to her feet. Fists on shapely hips, she scornfully appraised him from head to toe. She flipped her hair over her shoulders and headed for the door.

"I'm going back to my room. I doubt Linda's there yet, she's always luckier than me."

"I didn't mean to be so forward!"

Celia snorted. "You call that being forward? I can't wait to get to college where the boys know what to do. Goodbye, Will."

"It's Gil."

"Whatever."

Despite feeling like a fool, Gil was happy she was gone. He paced, trying to convince himself it was all for the best. When he found the right girl, it would be different. He would know how to act, and what to do.

He stared at the TV, but, never a fan, quickly lost interest. He thought about writing in his journal, which he had been doing pretty regularly through high school. But he decided the night's events were not something he wanted in print. He looked out his window and studied the city, but the lights were not as bright and exciting as before. He would be glad to move on.

He laid down and briefly closed his eyes, but it was the first night in his life he'd not slept in his own bed and everything felt strange, out of place. His mind filled with dizzying visions of the day—the craziest of his life. Leaving home, the failed tryouts, meeting Danny, driving the Trans Am, and finally the disaster with Celia. He kept coming back to that. Even though it seemed the most trivial. He decided he'd walk over to Danny's room and see if he had suffered a similar fate. Perhaps the sisters shared a mean streak.

The hallway was empty, and he stepped down two doors to Danny's room. He was about to knock when he heard sounds from within. He put his ear to the door and knew instantly what they meant. He blushed, and carefully backed away.

As he plodded to his room, he decided he would need to get some sleep. Tomorrow was going to come sooner than expected, and he had a long drive ahead of him.

To Gil's everlasting gratitude, Danny proved to be quite the gentleman and a true friend during the telling of the sad tale. He did not giggle, smirk, titter, or guffaw as they sped across the Chihuahuan Desert with Gil behind the wheel laying out all the dirty details. When the story was told, Danny leaned back, jaw clenching and proceeded to deride Celia in the most colorful fashion. It made Gil's heart warm knowing it was not only he who could feel such ire over a woman.

When he was finished with his tirade, the car fell silent. Gil thought he might have tired himself out with all the ranting, and was taking a well-deserved nap. But he was mistaken. So much so, he almost lost control of the car when Danny suddenly asked, "You a virgin, Gil?"

"What's it to you?!"

"I thought so. It's alright. Girls can get in the way."

"That's my thinking!"

Danny looked over at him. "I envy you, man. You've got more focus than fifty guys like me. I just never found anything I really care about that much."

Gil remained silent. He had never questioned why he was like he was. But now, he thought about it, and the answer soon came.

"Less than twenty-thousand have ever played in the majors. Over two-hundred thousand games in almost a hundred fifty years, and only that many got the chance. I aim to be one of them, Danny. As far as I can see, it's not gonna be possible if my mind's split."

Danny stared over, eyes flickering. "You're like a monk. Maybe that's what your nickname should be."

"Already got me one. G-Man."

Danny let it roll around his lips. "Hmm. Damn, I like that. Okay, G-Man, let's pick up the speed. Nothing out here but sand and you can see a cop five miles out. I want to get to Houston in plenty of time so we have all day tomorrow to get you ready for these next tryouts. One way or the other, we're going to get you in the show."

"Yesterday it was about both of us."

"Eh, I'll get what I need. And so will you. After you're in the bigtime, you won't be able to beat the babes off with a stick. Oh, G-Man!" he squealed in a falsetto. "I just love how you handle your bat!"

"Knock it off," said Gil, choking with laughter.

Danny placed a hand on his shoulder and laughed along with him, and as if by magic, the desert didn't seem quite so empty.

Chapter 9

"HELLO?"

"Hey mom . . . mom? Can you hear me?"

"Hello Gil. I didn't recognize the number."

"I figured you wouldn't. It's my friend Danny's phone. I borrowed it . . . mom, you there?"

"Tucker told me about him."

"I hoped he would, so you wouldn't worry. He's an alright guy. You'd like him."

"I'm glad."

"Sure don't sound like it. And you don't sound too happy to hear from me."

"I was hoping it would be before this."

"I know. I was waiting. Wanting to surprise you with good news. I still don't have any. But I called anyway."

"How nice of you."

"Aw, come on. Don't be like that. You knew I had to go eventually. Prescott had nothing left to offer."

"You should've told me about Coach Reynolds. I would have talked to him about letting you play."

"Wouldn't have made any difference! He's stuck in the mire."

"I still wish I'd have known."

"I didn't want you to get upset. And I'm sure you're not happy about me leaving school, but—"

"I don't give a damn about school, Gil! I understand you have to do what you have to do. It's just—never mind. It's late."

"I know. It's later here, because I'm three hours ahead of you, but I was waiting until you got off from work. How's it going in there, anyway?"

"It's just work. Not sure what I'm doing it for anymore."

"Everybody's got to work, mom."

"I used to think I was working for you. To give you a chance."

"And you did! Now it's time for me to pay you back."

"I never asked to be paid back, Gil."

"Aw, geez, don't cry."

"We used to be a team."

"We still are!"

"But you shut me out. Not even a note when you left."

"I thought you'd stop me from chasing this dream!"

"It used to be mine as well, remember?"

"Please mom! Stop crying!"

"I'm tired."

"Oh. Well, sure. I understand. Are you eating alright? Got to remember to eat."

"I have to go. Maybe you can write me a letter some time. Let me know where you're at. Be easier that way."

"Sure, mom! I will. And just so you know, right now, Danny and I are heading to Atlanta. There's another tryout there. I'm sure I'll be spotted in this one. Somebody out there has to notice me. Right, mom? Mom. You still there?"

Top of the 4th

I SAW AN OCEAN LAST WEEK. I thought I'd seen one when we were in Houston, but it was only the Gulf of Mexico. But it sure looked big. Seems like a lifetime since then, but it was only a couple months ago, with a bunch of tryouts along the way. Colorado, Kansas City, Milwaukee, and others I choose to forget.

Anyway, this ocean I saw in Florida was the Atlantic. And Danny was right. It was bigger and grander than anything I've ever seen. My eyes hurt from staring out at it. It seemed to have no end, just like this journey. I realize now, when I was a kid, I underestimated how hard this was going to be. Makes me laugh at myself now, how little I knew. Just like a toddler, thinking they can run before first learning to walk.

I've had a total of zero luck at these tryouts. No one will take me seriously about using both arms, no matter how hard I try to make them see the light. A couple coaches told me I should concentrate on my left arm. Maybe they're right, I've heard it before, but I'm not willing to give up yet.

One thing I've learned is there are a lot more people than I thought with the same dream as me. Thousands of them. Some are my age, but a lot are older. Some have even played in the minors, but for one reason or another, usually injury, they're back on the bottom of the heap, clawing to get back in the game. We all have the same look—hungry. That's what it is. I've come to where I can tell when a fella has just about given up. It's as if he hasn't eaten in a month. Starving. Desperate. I'm almost afraid to look at them for fear I'll see myself looking like that someday.

We're on our way to the nation's capital next. It should be interesting, the way Danny describes it with all these giant monuments of famous people. After that comes Cleveland, Chicago, and last stop, Boston (can't stand the Red Sox, but beggars can't be choosers). I've seen more of this country than I ever thought I'd see. But, as long as I'm on a baseball field, the world is the same everywhere.

The season is in full swing, so most teams are only looking for specialists to fill in the gaps. Seems to be no gap for me to fill so far. The worst thing is I'm dying just to play in a game. Any game. These tryouts are brutal. Ten pitches. That's it. If you ain't throwing lightning bolts, you're done. I'm afraid if I don't play a full game soon, I'll forget what it feels like, working the batters, finding the weaknesses.

Enough complaining. As Danny says, never say die. Well, I ain't dead yet, and I'm still moving on. It's been the craziest experience of my life, traveling with him. He sure likes to live good on his dad's money. Sometimes I feel guilty, since he won't even stand for me paying a nickel for anything. He's got to cover the whole tab, and I've been letting him. I still have all the money Tucker gave me, five hundred dollars. And most of the three hundred I brought along. Probably a good thing, as I feel my time living high with Danny is coming to a close.

He won't talk about it, but the tryouts are running out, and recently I've seen him several times on the phone with his father. His year of freedom is almost up, and I suspect he will return to California and do what is expected of him. I'm not sure what I'll do when that happens.

I've been using his laptop to study up on my options. When I was younger, I would never have considered the outlaw leagues, what they call independent ball. But right about now, I'll take what is given. They don't pay much, but it's said they can be a stepping stone to the majors, and I can't afford to overlook any options. Unfortunately, most have their short seasons in the summer, which doesn't help me since summer's already begun! There are some that play winter ball, specifically, the Mexican Pacific League. I can't picture myself in Mexico, though. Can't speak but a few words of the language, but maybe that doesn't matter. Baseball is baseball no matter where it's played.

Which brings me to a discovery I made. I always figured baseball was mostly an American thing. Boy, was I wrong. Seems they have leagues almost everywhere. Places like Germany, Italy, China, even someplace called Slovakia! Who'd have thought our game could spread so far. I haven't really looked into how to play with these leagues because I have absolutely no interest in going so far away, where it's damn sure I can't speak their languages either! But who's to say where this journey will lead me. Just in case, I do have a passport. My mom made me get one when I was sixteen. She claimed all Americans should have one, even if they never used it. Well, I've never used it, nor do I wish to! But I suppose it is a good thing to have handy.

Speaking of my mom, she isn't too happy with me, which makes it even more important to have some kind of success so I can make it up to her. I should have let her know what I was up to when I first left. It was a big mistake, and I don't know how to make it right other than prove to her I can do what I claim. I want so much to get her out of that crappy apartment it hurts just thinking about it. I wonder if she knows how I feel. Probably not, because I'm terrible at explaining myself.

Anyway, it would be wrong to say I haven't had any luck at all. Heck, it was a stroke of genius running into Danny. He's a lot of fun. I've seen places I would never have seen without him. I've slept in fancy hotels and eaten expensive food. And he talks real good, using all kinds of big words. We have a great time together. He's taught me a lot about girls. Even though I haven't had the success he has, I know someday the lessons will be put to good use. But that boy, well, he's like flypaper. The girls get stuck on him with one glance. If I were him, I'd be crowing from dawn to dusk, but he takes it in stride. Like it's all just natural, and to be expected.

One thing that bothers me is how concerned he is over my success, or lack of. He takes it as a personal failure when I'm not allowed to switch-pitch at the tryouts. I tell him it's not his worry, but he won't hear about it. I have become a "cause célèbre" for him, as he likes to say. Which is all fine, but it sure puts the pressure on me, knowing how much he cares. I kind of wish he'd worry more about getting himself on a team. I can tell he's not too thrilled at the idea of becoming a lawyer. Who would be?

Then again, maybe there is a bit of lawyer in him, because he's all the time going on about how it's wrong for the coaches not to let me do what I do best. And when he says the word wrong, it's like it's a sin. In fact, when he goes on a rant, he sounds like a preacher. He can sure put up an argument. And who am I to disagree? He's preaching to the choir. But, I've come to believe, despite his sermons, that just because something is wrong doesn't make it something you can change.

It's been a couple of weeks since I've talked with Tucker. The last call was pretty short. Not sure why. He and Mandy are doing good. I asked about when they were going to get married, and he said they hadn't planned anything yet. I get the feeling, though, something else is going on, but I can't put my finger on it. Maybe next time we talk, I can wheedle it out of him.

I don't know what else to write. I will say to all those reading this, if you ever set out on a journey like mine, make sure you know what you're up against. Then multiply that by ten. It's always going to be tougher than you think. One thing I didn't expect was how much I would miss out on. Tucker says high school graduation was a big deal, and there was an even bigger party afterwards. I miss being there. And I miss going fishing with Tucker, even though I really don't care much for fishing. And I miss cooking for my mom, and taking care of her.

It's things like that you don't count on losing when you set out on the path. Just remember the goal had better be worth it, because you don't get what normal people get. Life is just different. That's for damn sure. And I have a funny feeling in my gut, this is just the very beginning.

Chapter 10

As they skirted the Charles River, leaving Boston on Interstate 90, neither Danny nor Gil had anything to say. It was a sunny day, but the gloom in the car was palpable. The last tryout had gone like all the rest. No more chances, no more hope.

Gil was driving, and wondering what he was going to do with his life. To return to Prescott empty-handed was out of the question.

Option one. He could pick a city and have Danny drop him off. He would get a job, a cheap room, and wait out the fall and winter. Next year, he would try again.

Option two. He could try and get into a college. He noticed college players were having more success at the tryouts than those who hadn't attended. It was a sound idea, but one he knew was impossible. He had no money and no scholarship. Even if he did, he would have to take the GED exam first. And he wasn't at all sure he'd pass.

Option three. The Instructional Leagues. And there were a lot of them. The California Winter, Hudson River, South Florida Winter, and on and on. All offered to teach young players the ropes and show them off in front of scouts and managers.

It sounded great until he found out they actually charged money to participate. Often, more than $3000 for programs lasting less than a month. To Gil, the very notion of paying to play was distasteful. It was like buzzards feeding off the hopeful. Even if he had the money, he could not bring himself to play into that game.

Then there were the showcases, where top-notch scouts actively recruited and signed players. But, again, it all came back to the lack of college experience. In order to participate a player was required to have a college coach request an invite. No college, no go.

If there were other available options, Gil wasn't aware of them. Despite clearly seeing the goal in mind since he was a kid, it seemed he had taken all the wrong turns along the way. But there was nothing he could do about that. And for the first time since originally dreaming of being in the majors, his resolve was faltering. As the miles clicked by, the thought of giving up began to solidify in his mind. It would be easier, in some ways. If only he could learn to live with himself as a failure.

He was not aware of it, but Danny could sense what he was thinking. Perhaps it was the close bond the two travelers had formed that allowed one to know what the other was thinking. Or maybe it was just a lucky guess. Either way, twenty miles before the turnoff for Interstate 84, the first leg of their westward journey, Danny sat up straight.

"Pull over at the next exit," he said. "I'm driving."

"Was I speeding?"

"Nope. I'm taking a little detour."

Instead of turning onto 84, Danny stayed on 90, and in downtown Schenectady, they pulled into a hotel.

Coincidentally, it was another Double Tree Hilton. Surprisingly, despite the presence of several approachable girls lounging around the pool, Danny chose to look the other way. He was on a mission.

They spent the night enjoying a nice dinner and watching a movie in Danny's room. Gil's persistent probing, however, could not uncover where this detour was leading. Not that he cared so much. It was a reprieve from having to figure out what to do next. Also, his time with Danny was short, and he would dearly miss his companion. Any extra day with him was time well spent.

An hour into the drive the next morning, they approached a beautiful, crystal clear lake. The water glimmered, like a polished mirror reflecting the bright colors of the sailboats dotting its surface. Danny remained quiet, but as they drove the length of Otsego Lake, a grin formed.

They entered a small village that seemed as if time had passed it by, leaving a place more suited to the 19th century. There was only one traffic light, and no strip malls. A stately building came into view, Village Hall written in block letters across the top. In the front yard stood a wooden sign holder, advertising upcoming events sponsored by the Cooperstown Association.

Gil blinked. Read it again, and said, "Cooperstown."

"Took you long enough," said Danny.

"The Cooperstown?"

"Is there another?"

"I didn't know it was here!"

"What's wrong, Mr. Baseball Encyclopedia. I thought you knew everything."

"Well I knew it was in New York State. Just didn't know exactly where."

"Well now you know. And I thought since we were so close we might check out the Hall of Fame. Can you spare the time?"

"Can I spare the time, he asks! Of course I got the time! Come on, where is it?"

Danny pointed across the street, and there it was. Just like Gil had seen in pictures. They had barely pulled into a parking spot when he jumped out and took off.

The museum had just opened and a long waiting line ran around the left side of the main building. Gil and Danny took their place at the end of the queue. They were just off a grassy courtyard where stood two bronze statues. One of a pitcher, having just hurled a pitch, and several feet away, a crouched catcher, forever frozen, awaiting the ball.

"Do you know who they are?" asked Gil smugly.

"No. But I'm sure you can enlighten me," said Danny.

"That's the Dodger southpaw, Johnny Podres on the mound, and Roy Campanella at the plate. It's 1955, World Series, Game 7. Dodgers against the Yankees at Yankee Stadium. Podres threw a shutout to clinch the series. The game saw only two runs, an RBI single, and a bases loaded sac fly, both by Gil Hodges. That's who I'm named after. Did you know that, Danny? Well, anyway, it was the first World Series loss by the Yankees since '42 and only the second since '26. Roy won the National League MVP that year, and Johnny received the first ever World Series MVP. He won games 3 and 7, both complete games, with a 1.00 ERA. It was the first and only championship Brooklyn ever won. In '57 they moved to L.A. What a crying shame."

Several people in line who had been intently listening to this recitation, started cracking up, agreeing with Gil's lamentation over the infamous move to the West Coast.

An old man with his arm around a young boy, leaned into Gil and said, "Thank you for that, son. Memory's starting to go. I was at that game and I couldn't have explained it better to my grandson than you did."

Gil tipped his ball cap. "My pleasure, sir. And I sure do envy you. Wish I'd been there with you."

The line inched forward, but Gil and Danny waited patiently. When it was their time to buy tickets, Danny began to pay, but Gil slapped his hand away, firmly insisting he cover the tab this time.

The cashier waved them in, like ushering them past the pearly gates. To say Gil was in heaven, however, would be underestimating the sublime ecstasy he felt as he wandered through the halls and galleries. He knew these players like they were family. And, in a way, that's what they were.

There were sad moments, of course. At the Roberto Clemente display, tears rolled unchecked down his cheeks as he contemplated what might have been if the finest man ever to play the game had not died prematurely.

It was well past lunchtime—with no thought of food— when Gil saw Danny excitedly waving him over. He hurried to his friend and followed his eyes, landing on a six-finger glove. Gil's jaw literally dropped. He looked to Danny who had a wide grin on.

"That's Greg Harris' glove," stuttered Gil, in disbelief. "I had no idea. I mean, I figured they must have it here, but they only show you a little bit of all they got back in storage. Oh, man. This is something else. Just look at it. Look at it, Danny!"

"G'day mates," said a cheerful man with ruddy complexion who suddenly appeared at their sides. "What's got you fellas so gobsmacked?"

"What's that your talking?" asked Gil.

"The attraction! What do we got here? Oh, my. Fella that wore that sure got the bad break, eh? Born with six fingers. Don't know what I'd do if it happened to me. Kids at school must have really let him have it."

Gil scowled. "He don't have six fingers! His name's Greg A. Harris. He used it so he could move it from one hand to the other depending on what arm he was pitching with."

The man wrinkled his nose. "You're yanking my chain, aren't ya? Making fun of the poor Aussie, eh? A pitcher using both arms. Not possible."

Gil huffed. "It's called switch-pitching!"

The man held up both palms. "Alright now, settle petal. I just never heard of such a thing. And I never, ever saw a mitt like that. Must be one of a kind, eh?"

Gil rolled his eyes and Danny stepped in. "Actually, my friend here is a switch-pitcher, and he's got one of these gloves out in the car."

The man's eyes popped. "Well stone the crows! Would you believe that! What outfit you play for, mate?"

Gil looked away, but Danny quickly said, "We've been hitting the tryouts all summer. He's still keeping his options open."

The man's eyes narrowed knowingly. "Is he now. Well, I sure would like to see your friend in action. Must be a sight to see. Think maybe you could give us a demonstration, um—didn't get your name?"

"Gil Hayes. But I don't see a reason why I need to prove anything to you."

"No reason at all! It's just I was thinking what a hissy fit the other teams in our league would have if I showed up with a genuine switch-pitcher. That'd be heaps of fun—for us that is!" He slapped his sides and hooted loudly, drawing the attention of a security guard.

"What league are you talking about?" asked Danny, suddenly interested.

"Greater Brisbane, part of the Queensland crew. Talking about Australia, if you haven't caught on yet."

"And you're on one of the teams?"

"I should say so! Name's Noah Walker, pleased to meet you. I'm the head coach of the Toowoomba Rangers."

He stuck out a hand. Danny shook. "Name's Danny."

The man swung his hand to Gil, but he ignored it, chuckling to himself like it was all a silly joke. The man dropped his hand and his eyes twinkled playfully.

"Oh, you heard of us have you. Well, we're really not as bad as everybody says. Fact is, this year I think we're going to go all the way. Especially if we have a ringer like you. That is if you're as good as you seem to think you are."

Gil tightened his jaw and squared up to the man. "You saying I'm lying?"

"Easy on, mate. I don't want to have a barney with you. Just want to see you pitch."

They stared at each other for several moments. Danny broke in with, "Is this part of the Australian Baseball League?"

"Not exactly," said Noah, still holding Gil's stare. "The ABL is sort of like the MLB in this country. But the six state leagues, of which we're part of, function like your minor leagues. Fella does well in them, good chance he'll get picked up by one of the pro teams. A lot of your players are using Australia as a stepping stone."

Gil snorted. "What do Australians know about baseball? It's an American game."

"True as day, mate. But you might not know your miners brought the game over to our country as early as the 1850's. We've been playing ever since. Stands are always filled. We take it very, very seriously. Just like you, right?"

Gil remained silent, but Danny moved on. "So you have the power to draft Gil?"

"Heck yeah. Team will do whatever I say."

"What's the difference," said Gil. "Season's already halfway through."

"You're wrong, mate. Hasn't even begun. Our summer is your winter and the other way around. Season starts in October and runs nearly all the way to Easter."

Danny sized up the situation. "What kind of contract?"

Noah raised an eyebrow. "Well, like the old folks say, putting the cart before the horse ain't ya? First I'll need to see what your boy can do."

Danny eyed Gil. "What do you say, man? It's worth a try."

"Have any of the other tryouts been worth it?"

Danny found no response, and Gil turned away, signaling a desire to end this conversation.

Noah silently took in the moment. He politely cleared his throat and said, "I bet they're not taking you seriously, are they Gil? Probably won't even let you show your stuff. Sure, the powers that be will display one of these here gloves in their museum, but it's more an oddity than anything else. What you're up against in this country is tradition, mate. They don't like things being different than they always were. Am I close?"

Gil shrugged derisively. Danny nodded.

"Well, we have traditions in Australia as well. One of our most important ones is this: Win. No matter what it takes."

This grabbed Gil's attention and he studied Noah, finally liking what he saw.

Noah smiled back. "Now in my book, a pitcher who can toss with both arms is a weapon to be reckoned with, and as a coach, one I can't afford to pass by. All I need is a little sample of what you do."

"I won't be put off with ten pitches," said Gil firmly. "And I want to throw to batters."

"Good on ya, mate!" cried Noah, again riling the security guard. "Hang on a tick. Won't take but a sec to set this up."

Danny raised his eyebrows as Noah whipped out his cellphone. "How you going to round up a bunch of batters around here?"

"It's a cinch. My son is participating in the invitational tournaments just up the road in Dreams Park. He's just an ankle biter, way too young to play in our league, but he's coming along. Outfielder. Prefers center, but he needs to work on his throwing arm. Anyway, he's a real sport. He'll take care of everything."

Noah waited with phone to ear. "Liam, it's me . . . Your dad! Who do you think?" He cupped the phone. "He's a real jokester." He chuckled, and went back to the phone.

"Liam, listen, I want you to round up a bunch of batters, righties and lefties. No, not the younger boys, I need them to be older, the coaches, park employees, like that—Because I said so! I'm looking to try out a new pitcher for the Rangers. Of course I'm talking about an import! What else? You think I found an Aussie around here? Right. So, I want you to gather as many as you can, and we'll see what this guy's got. After supper, we'll use one of the fields way out back. Number eleven I think it is.

"What? Oh, bugger the organizers! All the games will be over for the day. Why should they care? Okay, good. Now make sure you get some sluggers. In particular, get that one coach, the big brute from Kansas with the attitude and the giant honker. Yeah, that one. And that swell black fella who brought the team of kids up from—I forget. Georgia, that's right. Get him. And whoever else is ready to tear it up. Oh, and bring along the fat kid on your team. Because we need a backstop! Don't ask so many questions. You got all that? Alright, I'll come over now and mosey around the fields during the games. Maybe I can find some dads who can still swing. Right. See ya later."

He hung up and looked to Danny and Gil. "It's down the road due south of here a click or two. You'll find it. I'll wait for you in the big parking lot. Say around seven?"

Danny looked to Gil, who nodded. Noah grinned. "This'll be fun, mates. Hooroo!" He waved and quickstepped out of the gallery.

Gil, in a daze, watched him go. He turned back to his hero's glove and stared through the glass. Danny, completely out of character, was nervous and fidgety, wondering what his friend was thinking. Minutes clicked by.

"Danny," said Gil, out of the blue. "Will you answer me one thing?"

Danny's stomach flip-flopped, wondering what was coming. "I'll do my best."

Gil cocked his head to his friend, dead serious. "Where in the hell is Australia?"

It took a beat, then Danny lost it. Roaring with laughter, he fell into Gil, clutching his shirt to keep from falling. Gil, missing the joke, looked down at him like he'd gone insane. The security guard headed their way.

Chapter 11

DREAMS PARK WAS VAST. Situated on 165 acres, it was its own village. It boasted 22 fields, a battery of batting cages, training facilities, and 104 clubhouses. There were dining pavilions, a retail center, train station, arcade, and a pond, to boot. The park operated all summer with a tournament each week featuring different teams from all over the country.

That evening, as they walked from the parking lot to one of the far-flung fields, Noah explained to Gil and Danny that each team had to have a minimum of 11 players. They could be put together as loosely as a bunch of neighborhood friends. Liam had joined a team from New Jersey because he and one of the players were online gaming pals, and the team was shy a player that year.

Danny was interested in Noah's description, but Gil was in the zone, barely hearing a word as he quieted his mind. He was not sure he was interested in going to Australia, but he was certain he was going to show this guy he could do what he claimed.

Earlier, after he and Danny left the Hall of Fame, they managed to find one hotel room. It was the first time they had to share a room, because the parents of the kids attending Dreams Park had snapped up almost all available lodging.

While they waited for their appointment, Gil could tell Danny thought he should jump at the opportunity to play in Australia—if he could pass muster. He assured Gil that despite the slang Noah used, the people really did speak English. So that was not a problem. Gil was unconvinced, and Danny backed off, watching him go through his juggling routine.

Now, it was time to go to work. And Gil was ready. The lineup consisted of four coaches, five college players who had summer jobs at the park, and three dads. Eight righties and four lefties. When Noah started to give introductions, Gil said, "Mr. Walker, no need for all that. I'm not going to spend enough time with these fellas to get to know them. Let's play ball."

Noah grinned and waved him to the mound. Liam and a few of his teammates took the field to shag balls. Their catcher squatted behind home plate.

Twenty-two minutes later, the tryout was over. It was almost anticlimactic. All the frustration over the failed tryouts was harnessed into a fierce determination to show who he was, and Gil's performance was nothing short of inspired.

There was one hit, an infield pop-up by the coach from Georgia which Gil fielded. He had switched arms four times and struck out eleven.

Danny had caught balls for Gil, but he'd never actually seen him pitch to batters. He had been going on blind faith, but as he watched his buddy mow down the lineup, he knew he was right not to doubt. Noah sat next to him during the pitching display, silent, in awe of what he was witnessing.

When Gil retired the last hitter he felt like he was just getting started. He waved to some of the earlier batters, egging them on for another try, but there were no takers.

Liam dashed from centerfield and slid to a halt in front of him. He was tall for the age of twelve, with the same complexion and bewitching grin as his father.

His eyes glistened as he stared at Gil. "Wow. A switch-pitcher. Who'd a thought it? My dad can sure pick 'em! You just pitched a four- inning no-hitter! The Rangers are a shoo-in this year with you on board. May I shake your hand, Mr. Hayes?"

Gil relaxed out of his zone, and smiled. "It's Gil. Pleased to meet you Liam."

"We have an extra bedroom since sis took off to college. It's right next to mine. So, I'm going to tell dad we have to be your host family. Boy, are we going to have fun, eh?"

"Host family?"

Danny hustled up, with Noah bringing up the rear. "Damn, G-Man!" cried Danny. "You sure weren't lying!"

Noah said, "So you already have a nickname. Too bad. I was going to call you the Terminator."

"Aw, come on," said Gil. "Those guys aren't pros. It was no big deal."

"If you say so," said Noah. "But it sure turned my head around. And barely nothing but junk pitches. Up, down, in, out, all around, everything moving every which way."

"I always figured pitching was more about brains than brawn," said Gil with a grin, having his secret discovered. "These days, with everybody looking for heaters, it's the only way to go. Plus, it saves wear and tear on the guns."

Noah laughed. "You're a swing reader, that's what you are. It's a lost art. And the offer's yours if you want to be a Ranger this year. Beats sitting around until next year's tryouts. And I guarantee you'll be in the starting rotation."

"Hold on," said Danny. "Now who's putting the cart before the horse? What kind of deal are we talking about?"

Noah chuckled. To Danny's keen ears, it sounded a little forced. "Well, first off, what other skills do you have, Gil? I mean other than baseball. What else can you do?"

Gil scrunched his face and looked to Danny, who said, "He can juggle."

"Interesting. But I was thinking a little more practical. You ever have a job?"

"Ever since I was a kid!" declared Gil. "Last one was at a diner in Prescott."

"What about Eli's place!" shouted Liam. "He could use him. His food is the pits."

Noah clamped a hand on Liam's shoulder, hushing him. "So you're a cook, eh?"

"Well, mostly I did prep, but I've been cooking for my mom since I could see over the stove. She always said I had the touch."

Noah grinned. "Perfect. Aussies love nothing more than good old-fashioned home cooking. So that settles it." He and Liam beamed at Gil like they'd hit the jackpot.

Gil shook his head, trying to make sense of this. Danny narrowed his eyes and put on his lawyer cap. "I think you better lay out all the details of the contract."

Noah swallowed hard, his Adam's apple bobbing nervously. "Contract. Right. Okay, here's how it works. We'll set you up with a place to stay and all the food you can eat."

"You betcha!" shouted Liam. "Mum's a great cook!"

Noah looked at him. "He's staying with us then?"

Liam slapped him on the arm. "Of course, dad. Geez."

Noah shrugged. "Right. Anyway, for transportation, someone on the team always has a car available and you're welcome to it—"

"That's all fine, but what about the pay?" asked Danny, cutting him off.

"Well, now that I know Gil can cook, we'll get him a job at one of the other player's restaurant. He'll mostly pay you under the table to avoid any trouble with your visa."

"I was talking about the pay for playing," said Danny, scowling.

"Sorry, mate, these aren't pro teams," explained Noah with a worried frown. "We don't pay any of our players. Just the way it is."

Danny stared at him for half a beat, then said, "My mistake, Gil. I thought this guy was for real."

He turned to go and Gil laid a hand on his shoulder. "Hold on, buddy. Mr. Walker, about how much would it cost a person to get an apartment where you live?"

"If it's nothing special, I'd say anywhere from six to seven hundred dollars."

"And the food won't cost me nothing?" asked Gil.

"Not a cent."

"So, in a way, you really are paying me to play. You just have to go about it a different way."

"Spot on, mate! That's the way to look at it!"

Danny started pulling Gil away. "We're not interested."

Gil held his ground. "And that money I make cooking. That's all mine."

"Of course!" said Noah. "Every fella needs a few pineapples in their pockets for this and that, playing around, you know."

Gil looked at Danny. "It's not so bad when you get down to it. At least I'll get to play this winter, rather than just sitting on my butt. If you have any other ideas, I'm all ears."

Danny opened his mouth, but he was tapped out. "I just don't like people with talent getting a raw deal. And what about the majors?"

"I haven't forgotten the goal. It's just I need to play. Real bad. It's like I haven't eaten in I don't know how long. And after I show these Aussies how the game is played, I'll be back. You can count on that."

"Gawd I love your style, Gil!" said Noah, beaming. "You talk like a winner."

"So you're going to join the team then?" asked Liam, bouncing up and down.

"I expect so," said Gil with a smile. "But it's a long way, isn't it? How will I get there?"

Noah's smile evaporated. "Plane ticket's on you, mate. That's just how it's done."

"Wait a minute!" cried Danny.

"How much does that set a person back?" asked Gil, ignoring Danny's outburst.

"Our tickets ran right around $1500 each, roundtrip," said Noah.

Gil's shoulders slumped. "Shoot. Well, I guess I'll have to pass then. But I understand why it's my responsibility to get myself over there."

"Well I don't!" shouted Danny.

"Steady on, mate," said Noah. "You have to realize, the Rangers are a non-profit organization. Any money we get we put towards the little ones, like Liam here. Teach them the love of the game, get 'em uniforms. All the teams work that way."

"Not all, dad," said Liam. "The bigger teams like the Bulldogs and Lightning cover the tickets for their imports."

Noah sighed, a little perturbed. "Thanks so much for correcting me, son. But like you said, those teams have got the big bucks. Not like Toowoomba. Fact is, Gil, you'd be the first import we've ever had."

"Is that a good thing?" asked Gil. "I mean, what's an import?"

"An American! Like you," said Liam. "All the teams want them, and the ones that have them always seem to win more than the rest."

"He's right," said Noah. "But it's just the way it is. If you've got the money, you get the best players. The Rangers just can't afford it."

Danny locked eyes with him. "And what about you, Coach? You look to be doing pretty well. Brought your son to this fancy camp. Can't be cheap. You want your team to win this year, why don't you cover the ticket?"

"Me!"

"Come on, dad!" cried Liam. "Your business is booming. Everyone in town says you're the one with all the bickies. They say you're just rolling in them."

"You talk too much, Liam!" snapped Noah. "Look, Danny. I know you want the best for your boy, but—"

"And you want the best for your team, right Coach?" said Danny. "So you want a ringer, then put up or shut up."

Noah chewed on his lip. Danny said, "Come on, Gil. This guy's not serious."

He yanked Gil and they started away. As they cleared the field, Gil said, "Geez, I hate walking away from this. Maybe I could work out some sort of deal. I still have nearly $700. That's almost half a ticket."

"No. That's your poker stake, Gil. Never spend it. Someday, when you least expect it, you're going to need it. Just keep walking. And don't look back. Trust me."

They were passing the batting cages when they heard, "Where the heck are you going, mates!"

Danny winked at Gil, and turned as Noah and Liam rushed up. Noah caught his breath and looked at Gil. "You've got yourself a real agent there. I'd hold onto him if I were you."

"So you'll cover the ticket? Roundtrip?" asked Danny.

"Well, how's this grab you. If you cover the ticket now, when Gil finishes the season, I'll make sure the team reimburses you."

Danny thought about it. "You going to put that on paper?"

"Sure! Anything you say."

Danny nodded. "Alright, we'll need to—"

"No!" shouted Gil. "I won't have you covering for me anymore. This is my problem."

"I get it, Gil," said Danny. "But you don't have the cash. This is the only way."

"Well then, I won't play. Sorry Mr. Walker. I just can't take money from my friend. I hope your team does well. I'll keep my fingers crossed. Come on, Danny."

"Dammit boys! Stop walking away. My goodness, you drive a hard bargain. But now that I've seen you pitch, G-Man, I'm hooked. I just gotta have ya. So, I'll put up the scratch for the ticket on one condition. You play the entire season with the Rangers."

Gil cocked his head in confusion. "Who else would I play for?"

"The ABL, that's who. Our Major League, remember? And I know once one of their teams spots you, they'll be trying to snatch you up for their short season."

"Yeah! The Brisbane Bandits, Adelaide Bite, they're famous for taking away our best players just when we need them," added Liam.

"Right," said Noah, "And if the team's going to invest all this money in you, we can't have you waltzing away when the going's tough. If you paid your own way over there, I'd have nothing to say about it. So that's the trade-off. Can you live with it?"

Gil immediately started to agree, but Danny stopped him mid-sentence. "You understand what you'll be risking, don't you? You could have a chance to play in the top league in Australia, and you'll have to turn it down. All because of a plane ticket."

Gil puckered his brow. "It's not about the ticket. When I sign up for a team, that's who I'm loyal to no matter what. And I aim to take the Rangers all the way this year."

Noah cried, "You are fair dinkum, mate, and I'll swear to it!"

Gil said, "Yet again, I have no idea what that means, but I'll take it as a compliment. And I appreciate the plane ticket, but I'll be paying you back when I can."

"You will do no such thing!" barked Danny.

"I'm serious, pal. No coach should have to fork out his own money."

Noah shrugged. "No worries. I'm sure I'll get it back from the organization."

"That's your business. But I'll cover my own debts out of my cooking money. And if you need anyone to help teach them young boys, I'm your man. I have a knack of explaining the finer details of the game."

"I'll just bet you do!" cried Noah. "And I'll definitely take you up on it. That's one thing the team can legitimately pay you for. But I'm not holding you hostage over that ticket. I just want you to pitch the way I saw today."

Gil shrugged. "That's no problem. Fact is, I felt a little rusty out there."

The others howled with delight. Noah slapped Gil on the back and said, "Now, our season starts in October, but we'll need to get you over earlier to practice with the team, and get you set up with the job. When do you think you'd like to fly?"

Gil was perplexed. "Thing is, Mr. Walker, I got nothing else going, and nowhere I need to be. So if it's alright with you, now would be good."

It took a second to register, then a wide smile spread on Noah's face. "Now would be excellent. But if you keep calling me Mr. this and Mr. that, we're going to have a problem. I'm just Coach."

"Alright, Coach," said Gil. He stuck out his hand and they shook.

"What about a visa?" asked Danny.

"No worries. We can apply for one online tonight. It's called the working holiday visa and it's good for a year. And I know exactly how to fill it out and vouch for Gil so they'll be no delay. You have a passport, don't you?"

"Course. Who doesn't?"

"You do?" asked Danny in disbelief.

"Wipe that silly look off your face, Mr. Know-It-All. You don't know everything about me. And just because I'm a yokel, don't mean I'm backward. My mom always said every modern American should have a passport, even if they don't use it."

Noah laughed. "Smart, mum you got there. And won't she be proud that you're using it now! Because in a very short time, you're going halfway around the globe."

Gil's eyes widened. He shot Danny a look. "You didn't tell me it was that far!"

"Surprise, surprise, Mr. Modern American," said Danny with a smirk. "Welcome to the real world."

Chapter 12

THE THREE SAT AROUND THE KITCHEN TABLE. Alice's face was stony and Tucker couldn't make out what she was thinking. Mandy held the letter but had not yet opened it. She found it in the mailbox that afternoon, and decided it was best to wait until Alice returned from work.

After graduating high school, Mandy had moved upstairs to live with Tucker. Alice had approved, realizing these two were inextricably tied together—now more than ever. Mandy's mother had also consented, but urged them to tie the knot as soon as they could afford their own place. Privately, Alice was happy for the company and was in no hurry to have them move out.

Mandy nervously toyed with the envelope. There was a strange tension in the room. Everyone was excited to know the contents, but at the same time, scared to find what had become of their Gil.

Tucker could take it no longer. "Dammit, come on, Mandy. Read it why don't you."

Alice nodded with just a slight tip of her head, and Mandy used her fingernail to slice through the top of the envelope. She removed the letter, carefully smoothing it out like fine linen, then leaned in and began to read.

"Hey everyone. It's me! But I guess you caught on to that already. Though I bet you'll never guess where I am. Well, maybe you will since you've no doubt seen the postmark. That's right. I'm in Australia! Toowoomba to be exact."

"Oh, my god," whispered Alice.

Tucker reached over and placed a hand over hers. "Go on, Mandy."

"Mom, I decided to listen to your suggestion and write this letter rather than call, as I know my last one upset you some. And I'm sorry for that. I hope this is a better way to communicate. The last thing I want to do in this world is upset you."

Alice abruptly stood and turned her back to the table, her jaw quivering, eyes welling up. Tucker silently bade Mandy to continue.

"Anyway, if I told you everything that has occurred it would fill up a telephone book. So, I'll do a recap. I ended up getting drafted by an Australian team to play winter ball. It doesn't pay much, but I figured I had to start somewhere. I had hoped the tryouts would go better, but maybe next year. Anyway, I'm not complaining. The people over here are real nice, and make me feel right at home."

A little burst of sound came out of Alice as she choked back tears. Tucker rose and held her shoulders. She nodded and said, "Go on, Mandy."

"It's not like real home. That would be impossible since my favorite people aren't here. But you can't have everything. I'm staying at the Coach's house which is real comfortable. And the mom, Chloe, acts like I'm just one of the family. My job is right down the street at a place called

Eli's Eats. Which makes sense since the owner's name is Eli. Ha Ha!

"But I guess I'm starting backwards. The deal is all my expenses are covered, which works as my pay for pitching. Then they set me up with this job so I can make some extra money. And believe it or not, I'm actually one of the main cooks already! The money's not great, but I don't have much to buy since everyone treats me so good. Danny and I split up when I took this offer, and he's off to college. But I'll always remember him for what he did for me, and I miss him bad."

Alice, eyes bleary, turned to Tucker and mumbled, "How did he manage this?"

Tucker shrugged. "He's got his sights set, Al. I imagine it's the only choice he had for now. You know he has to pitch no matter what."

Her eyes drooped, she nodded, and he helped her back into her seat.

Mandy continued. "The season hasn't started yet. Won't for a while. But the team has been practicing a couple times a week. Not as much as we need, though. I'm afraid we're not real good yet. So, even though none of us are real religious, when you get the chance, say a little prayer for the Toowoomba Rangers. And, Tucker, I could sure use you here to catch for me. This fella they got just can't seem to block my breaking balls, and it sure would be sweet seeing your face behind the mound."

Tucker's shoulders twitched. He put a fist to his mouth, and waved Mandy on.

"I know you all think I'm half a lunatic for doing this, but I see it as a real chance to better my game. And one thing for sure, they're as crazy for baseball as we are, maybe more so. All they talk about is winning, and that's easy for me to understand. I'm going to do my best to help them.

"The season goes almost to Easter, and after that I expect I'll be coming home. I forgot to tell you, part of the deal was I got my plane ticket covered both ways so I'm not permanently stuck here. It sure is a long way away. And it's a real change from Arizona. First off, it rains quite a bit more. In fact, they have this National Park right by that has what's called a rainforest. The whole family and I went to visit last week and it was something else. There was a big waterfall and huge granite boulders, just like the ones coming up Iron Springs Road! The town is known as the Garden City because everything grows so well here. Speaking of which, next month in September they have this thing called the Carnival of Flowers. I know you'd like that Mandy. You always were real fond of flowers. I remember you picking dandelions saying they were so beautiful. That always made me laugh how you could see a weed as something special. Maybe that's why you think my boy Tucker is such a handsome hunk. Ha Ha!"

Mandy laughed and Tucker blushed. Alice impatiently tapped the table, wanting more despite herself.

Mandy read on. "I hope everything is good with you two, and you're still as much in love as I remember. There never were two people so meant for each other. That's a fact. I hope you can hold off getting hitched until I come back. I sure would like to see that. But the most important thing is not to worry about me. I'm just fine. Especially when I take the mound. Sometimes, though, even with all these friendly people around, I feel alone just thinking of all of you. Hurts my gut some when I think too much about it.

"Well, I'm running out of paper and the family is going to take me to the beach today. It's only a couple hours away near some city named Brisbane. It should be fun, even though I'm not crazy for laying out in the burning hot sand all day.

"I sure hope you all can find time to write back. The address is on the envelope, and I'm going to write down the phone number of the house here in case there's an emergency. I'm sure it's expensive to call, and from what I can make out, we're like a day ahead of you. Though I'm not sure how that works. Okay then. I'll end by sending out my love, hugs, kisses and best wishes! Gil.

"P.S. Mom, I sure do owe you for making me get that passport. It sure came in handy! And I owe you for a lot more. For giving me my life, and always telling me I would succeed. That's what keeps me going. And I aim to pay you back for everything, no matter how long it takes."

Alice shoved back her chair and stumbled into her bedroom. Mandy carefully folded the letter and slowly looked up at Tucker.

"We need to write him right now. Tell him about the baby we're having. Tell him we're going to be married. He'll have to come back then."

Tucker shot to his feet. "We'll do nothing of the sort!"

"But Tuck, look at Al, it's killing her! And don't you miss him?"

"Of course I miss him! But we force him back here and we won't have the Gil that left. All we'll have is a caged animal. Not you, me, or Al's going to clip his wings. It would kill the dream. That's something we all share. And whether we like it or not, we're in this for the long haul."

Chapter 13

GIL TOSSED OFF TWO MORE PITCHES to the bullpen catcher and signaled that both his arms were ready—just in time. Far off across the green, the manager was holding up both arms as he walked to the mound to yank the pitcher.

As Gil trotted across the field, he could have no way of knowing this half inning, a mere 11 minutes, would be the start of an odyssey he could never have imagined in his wildest dreams.

By all accounts—and existing contracts—he should not have even been where he was. It all began a couple days before Christmas, when the phone in the Walker household rang.

"I got it!" cried Liam, dashing from the sofa.

Gil wondered if maybe it was his mother or maybe Tucker, wishing him a Merry Christmas. A couple letters had gone back and forth, but a call would be a much-needed treat. Noah was moping, as he had been since the start of their season. No amount of praying—or Gil's outstanding pitching—seemed to help the hapless Rangers. The boys just couldn't hit the ball and there had been little to no run support. Even with over two months left in their season, they had no hope of reaching a playoff berth.

"Who is this?" asked Liam. "I already said he's here. But I want to know who this is? Oh. Sure, I know who you are. Well, he's real sick. That's right. Caught a flu bug or something. It's just terrible! He might not make it through the week."

"Liam! What in the blazes are you talking about?" shouted Noah.

"It's the GM for the Brisbane Bandits, dad! He's trying to steal Gil!"

Noah sighed, as if expecting the call. "Well, let him talk to him."

"But, dad—"

"Now!"

Liam glared at the phone with unconcealed loathing then grudgingly handed Gil the phone. "Hello? Yes sir, it's me. What's that? Well, thanks, I appreciate it. Uh-huh. That's nice of you to offer, but I'm obligated to the Rangers for the rest of the season. No sir, I don't go back on a deal. Uh-huh. Well, I sure do wish the best for your team, but—"

Noah appeared in front of him with a strange look on his face, one that Gil could not read. "Mind if I talk to him for a moment."

"I sure wish you would, Coach. He's kind of pushy. Not sure how to handle it."

Noah smiled fondly at his ace, and took the phone. "This is Noah Walker. What can I do for you? Yeah, of course I've been watching your club. It's been a good year. Uh-huh. I agree, it can get dicey this part of the season. What's that? No, he's not as good as you think he is. He's better. Uh-huh. No. I wouldn't hold him back, if that's what he wanted. Yes. I'm willing to waive any agreement we made."

"Dad! Have you gone fruit loops?!" cried Liam.

Noah stomped his foot and waved him away. "As I said, that's up to him. But he's got my blessing. Sure. Just a sec. Here he is."

He held out the phone to Gil. "Coach. I don't understand. We made a deal."

"That's true, Gil. But nothing you can do is going to save us this year. You know it, and I know it. And look at it this way. If you help this team take the championship, it'll be a real feather in our cap. You'll be doing it for Queensland and everybody will know the Rangers are the ones that discovered you. And besides, it's only for a little over a month. You'll be able to finish up the season with us."

Gil frowned. "That always seemed a little backwards to me in this country. The minors having a longer season than the majors. But I still can't do it. I haven't paid you back in full for the plane ticket."

"Bugger the ticket, Gil. The team already paid me back. In fact, I've been socking away that money you've been giving me, with every intention of giving it back, with interest. Truth is, you've done everything I asked. And I've been feeling like crap knowing I brought you over here to play on a losing team. You'd be doing me a favor going to the ABL. At least I'd know you got something good out of all this. Who knows, might be some important scout out there will catch sight of you. You're sure as hell not going to get that in Toowoomba."

Gil stared hard at him. "Coach, I came over here for one reason. And that's to take the Rangers all the way. If it'll make you feel better, I'll go try and help these fellas, but on one condition. You bring me back next year so I can finish the job."

Noah laughed. "Gil, if the rest of the world is so blind they can't see the genius standing in front of me, and you're still available next year, of course you've got a place on the team! But either way, you'll always have a home here, no matter what."

Gil looked at the phone, and hesitated.

"Go on, mate. Give it a burl. You won't regret it."

And so here he was, jogging across the field in the middle of a hotly contested game between the Brisbane Bandits and the Canberra Cavalry. It was the end of January, and each needed the win to advance to the playoffs. Bottom of the eighth, score tied, men on first and third for the Cavalry, little wind, high humidity, no outs.

For the month Gil had been on the team, the Bandits had elected to use him as a specialist out of the bullpen rather than a starter. It didn't bother him. As long as he had the chance to pitch—and switch. So far, he had performed above expectations.

His success was in part due to his ongoing evolution as a pitcher. He had recently begun varying where he placed himself on the mound—sometimes a little left or right of the rubber depending on the pitch and arm he was using. This shifted the arm slot and threw off the batters. He had seen Zack Greinke do it as he got older and slyer, and it was paying off. He was currently carrying a 1.05 ERA, and was a force to be reckoned with. The ABL was not used to having a switch-pitcher in their ranks, but they had adapted with typical Aussie enthusiasm.

The manager plopped the ball in his hand, and with a wink and nod, took off for the dugout with no further instructions. Gil knew what was expected of him. And, as always, the task did not faze him. Nor did the large crowd, and constant din. He let his mind go silent and slipped into the familiar zone that batters had learned to dread.

As he methodically dismantled the first two hitters, a man seated behind home plate watched with keen interest, making quick notes in a little, black book. When Gil switched arms for the third batter, however, the man sat bolt upright. He had never seen such a thing and his mind raced with the possibilities. The half inning came to an end when Gil struck out the final batter, stranding the runners.

The score was still tied going into the ninth, but the man left his seat and scurried into the concession area to make a long-distance call. When he returned, it was just in time to see the closer for the Bandits give up a home run to blow the game and eliminate the team from the playoffs. He waited for the celebration by the Cavalry fans to die down, then he worked his way around to the outside of the arena where the players for both teams would depart.

He spotted Gil and made his move. He had pitch black hair, a large mustache, and spoke with a thick accent, but one Gil found strangely compelling. His sales pitch was equally intriguing. He represented the Rangers Redipuglia, an underdog within the Italian Baseball League. The team was desperate to win a championship and would spend whatever it took to win it this year. He said they needed Gil to help them do it.

Gil thought it was almost a sign from above the team shared the same name with Toowoomba. But this was pro ball, and for the first time in his budding career, he was offered real pay for playing, plus lodging, meals, and plane ticket. The season kicked off in April, so there would be almost no time off from playing—something that carried huge appeal. He already had it in mind to play for Noah the next winter, to finish what he had started, and this opportunity would allow him to keep sharp until then. There was no real drawback, except he would miss the American tryouts.

He wished Danny was there to help him decide, but he had a feeling he knew what he would say. Ultimately, his decision was made when he saw the desperate hope in the man's eyes. For some reason, he was convinced Gil could be the turning point for his long-suffering club. Gil knew this team needed him, and who was he to turn away.

He agreed on the spot. He was overwhelmed by the man's reaction. He hugged him and waved his hands excitedly in the air, like he was thanking God and Mother Mary for the gift that had been bestowed. Gil was red-faced by the time he was through, knowing some of the other players were watching this spectacle. After preliminary arrangements were made, the man departed.

Another import, Bobby, from Illinois, who played with the Cavalry, approached Gil and found out what had happened. "Lucky dog," he said. "Everybody wants to play in Italy. The bats are wood, competition is mean, and the women are friendly. Can't ask for more. Good luck to you, Gil. Maybe I'll see you back here next year. Depends on how the tryouts go for me in the States."

Gil wished him luck and headed for the bus back to Toowoomba, all the way home wondering just how much stranger this journey would become.

Predictably, despite the reinfusion of Gil's pitching, Toowoomba fell short of the playoffs. Noah was disappointed, but excited over Gil's decision to play in Italy and not attend tryouts, as it most likely meant he would be back for the winter.

The summer in Italy was a success. With Gil's help, the Rangers Redipuglia made it to the playoffs for the first time ever. They lost in the second round, but finally earned some bragging rights and the other teams had to pay closer attention. Gil met a few imports who played with the other Italian teams, and they formed a little gang, exploring the countryside on their days off.

Most of the natives didn't speak English—or chose not to, but there was this girl, Camilla, who lived next door to Gil's host family. She helped him learn a little Italian—and taught him a few other things, besides. So in the end, he also earned bragging rights that summer. Of course, he was not the sort to crow about his private doings with a woman. But he wished he could tell Danny he had finally graduated, so to speak.

At the end of July, on the next to last game, he was approached by a scout from the Czech Republic, claiming the team he represented was an up-and-coming powerhouse in the European League. He was so impressed by Gil's pitching he offered him a roster spot for the next summer. Gil was not ready to commit, because, frankly, he had no idea where this country was and he could barely understand what the man was saying! But he took his number, promising he would contact him if interested. He had thoughts of returning home before the start of the Australian season, but he felt if he was going to take the Rangers all the way this year, he should urge the team to start practicing early.

He had not been back at the Walker residence more than a week, when a call came from the manager of the Pine Hills Lightning, another team in the Queensland League. Gil was surprised at the man's gall, calling him at Noah's house, and he told him so. The manager was undaunted, promising him nicer accommodations, a better side job, the stars, the moon, and on and on, if only he would change colors and play with them. Gil hung up on him, but not before letting him know he relished the chance to beat the pants off the Lightning when they met up with the Rangers that season.

And that's exactly what happened. Toowoomba got off to a quick start and didn't look back. Mid-season, the Brisbane Bandits came knocking again, but Gil flat out turned them down. There was an undeniable buzz surrounding his team, and he was not going to walk out on the show. It was a good thing he didn't. Because for the first time ever, the Toowoomba Rangers won it all, taking the Australian Pacific League Championship with Gil pitching a three-hit shutout in the final game.

Scouts from the Netherlands and Croatia saw the game and both vied to get Gil's commitment to play with them. But after doing some research on European ball, Gil had already contacted the man from the Czech Republic. The Netherlands was a strong team, and Croatia was coming along, but his love of underdogs drew him to the Czechs. And so shortly after the end of the season, he hopped onto another plane, going to a place he had never seen, with a name he was still having difficulties spelling.

Bottom of the 5th

I HAVE FOUND TEACHING PEOPLE WHAT I DO is a real good way to figure out what I do. All these clubs I've been playing for get a real kick out of the fact I can explain the ins and outs of pitching. Most of the time I can't even speak their language, but it's clear to me now that baseball has a language all its own that crosses borders. And you don't really need many words to show a pitcher a certain grip and arm slot, then watch his eyes gleam when he sees how they affect the path of the ball.

Of course, there's no way to really explain how to know what pitch to throw at any given time or batter. I try to tell them it's just something you sense. It's always come natural to me, and I'm not sure it can be learned. I guess way back in Cooperstown, Noah put it best when he said I was a swing reader. I wasn't sure then what he meant by that, but I've come a long way. And he's right. I just seem to be able to know what the batter is waiting on, or wanting. Then it's an easy matter to throw something he didn't see coming. I know it frustrates catchers since they also don't know what I'm going to do. But I've worked around that by coming up with signals from the mound, so things kind of work in reverse with me calling the pitches rather than the catcher. They wouldn't like that in the States, but it works here.

I guess Noah was also right by saying I was a junk pitcher, and I've come to accept that. There have been plenty of famous pitchers who threw the same. Vic Raschi, "The Springfield Rifle," comes to mind, among others. I just never found it necessary trying to blow away batters with heat when it's a whole lot easier letting them strike themselves out flailing away at garbage. Plus, with me playing year-round ball, it's almost become necessary in order to save my arms from injury. I see too much of that in organized ball. By the time these poor pitchers are in their early twenties, they're wiped out from throwing lightning all the time. I urge anyone reading this who's planning on a baseball journey of their own to take this to heart. You don't have to hurt yourself to be good, it just takes a little brainpower. So many pitchers I see spend years off to have surgery, and by the time they get back, they're all used up. Not me, brother. I'm going to last as long as it takes to get where I'm going.

Speaking of which, I'm writing this on a plane bound for the Dominican Republic. I'll be playing winter ball there. It all came about in a funny way. A while back, after I finished summer ball with the Czechs which went real good, I was all set to go back to Australia and play with the Rangers. But after winning it all the year before, a lot of the older players figured to quit while they were ahead. This left Noah in a terrible spot, and he decided to drop the Division A team, and concentrate on his lower divisions. Build up a new top team from scratch. He said that was going to take time and was not worth my while playing in the lower divisions. I expect he was right, but it was sad having to leave.

I thought about going home, but Noah put in a call to the Melbourne Aces and let 'em know I was available. They snapped me up and I played the entire ABL short season that winter. We did pretty good, and I had a string of starts that caught the eye of a scout for the Kiwoom Heroes, one of the teams in the Korean Baseball League, or KBO. I had no idea they even knew what the game was. Was I wrong! Those people are gaga over the sport. Their season runs almost the same as our majors, and the stadiums are always packed. Not to mention they have the best players I've come up against since I left home. The fans really took to me. They even made little white pennants with G-Man printed in gold on them, and when I took the mound the stands were one solid curtain of my nickname flapping in the wind. The team wants me back for next winter, but I'm counting on being signed with an MLB team by then.

But I sure liked my time in Korea. There were quite a few imports to pal around with and see the country. And the people are great once you get to understand how their minds work. I had a little help on that end. It came from a girl named, Jung-sook (I wouldn't kid you about that!). She showed me around, and explained the culture, and, well, taught me a bunch of other stuff, too.

She's a beautiful girl, and we got along real good. It was tough to say goodbye. But that's the curse you get when you set out chasing a goal. You can't stay one place too long, and you can't hang onto the people you'd like to. It's been nearly four years since I left home. I've come to think of it like my baseball college. Just paying my dues. And there's no denying I'm better than I was when I thought I was hot stuff. I've done the math, and so far, I'm stringing along a 1.28 ERA. Which is respectable anywhere in the world. Of course, I've had to adapt. Mostly by expanding the type pitches I throw.

If you combine both arms, I can now hurl a splitter, sinker, slider, screwball, change, curve, slurve, cutter, palmball, and I'm working on a nasty forkball. And, yes, yes, I've got a fastball. A four-seamer. It's not real fast, but I don't need much on it to set up my other stuff. Heck some of my pitches are so slow, the batters have time to lace their shoes before the ball gets to the plate! My slow curve barely cracks 65 mph. And though I haven't had the chance to use it, I've even mastered the Eephus pitch that old Rip Sewell invented. Some people call it the blooper ball and for good reason! Well, that dang thing doesn't nearly top 45 mph with a tailwind! I'll keep that one up my sleeve for the right occasion. What a surprise that will be for some unlucky batter!

So many of these teams don't like the fact I pitch with both arms. About drives them to distraction at times. But that's none of my concern. They've just had to learn to put up with it. I'm a switch-pitcher. And no one is going to tell me otherwise.

Anyway, to explain why I'm on this plane. When I was in Korea, an international scout touted me to a bunch of teams he represents and I was picked up by the Tigres del Licey. And when I try to pronounce that, I about choke on my tongue! The scout said it is a great privilege to play in this league as many players end up going to the majors. Fact, I wouldn't even have been chosen if I hadn't acquired what they call verifiable stats playing for the ABL, KBO, and in Europe. He says it's a big stepping stone for my career. I sure hope so. I'm a little weary of baseball college and am ready to graduate.

I'm not the only one. My mom is about fed up with me. She won't say so directly, but I can tell. When I wrote her and said I was coming back to that part of the world, she informed me if I didn't come visit, there would be hell to pay. And nobody wants to mess with Ice when she gets like that. Tucker was a lot less harsh. He's real excited to see me. Says he has all kinds of surprises. I can hardly imagine.

From what I understand, they're fixing to throw me a birthday party this spring. I'll be twenty-one, though I feel older. Mom says she's got the perfect gift for me, and I damn well know what it is. A phone. I really don't want one. But I have the notion it will not be up for debate. And I guess she's right. When any of my teammates find out I don't have one, they act like I'm from another planet. People sure do put a lot of stock in those damn things. But I guess it's time for me to surrender.

What none of the family knows, is I've been saving up almost every dollar I've made over these years. And I still have my original poker stake folded up in my wallet. The exact same bills. Danny said I should hang onto it, and I haven't forgotten. But, except for that, and a little traveling money, I'm going to give everything else I've made to mom. It's not a whole lot for four years work, but I hope it will be enough to get her a new place to live. It's what this is all about, anyway. Why else would I be doing it? Or maybe it's better the other way around. What else would I be doing?

I admit, it will feel strange being back in my own country. I've enjoyed living with different people from around the world, and I must be an okay guest, since all my host families have been sad to see me go. And, believe it or not, I've been so many places, I had to get what's called an insert for my passport, because the pages were all filled up with visas. Who would have thought I'd become such an experienced world traveler.

It's been a habit of mine to pick up new recipes wherever I am, and with sometimes cooking professionally, I now have quite the selection I can whip up. I can't wait to see what new specialties I can find in the Dominican Republic. I'll be staying with the Fuentes family, and I'll be sure to nose around the kitchen to see what's cooking.

I'm flying over an ocean right now. Not sure which one. Never even knew there were so many. Whichever it is, it sure is big. Endless. Just keeps going on and on. Forever and a day.

Chapter 14

TUCKER PICKED HIM UP AT THE AIRPORT. It was early March. Gil thought he'd be back earlier, but his team had been one of the top four in the Dominican League, and in January, after the regular season ended, they moved into a round-robin 50-game playoff. They finished as one of the top two teams and played a final best-of-nine series to see who would win the national title. The Tigres won and in February represented the country in the Caribbean Series. The match was held in Venezuela, and after a tight battle, Cuba took home the honors.

The two friends came together like they'd never been apart. Tucker, never one to waste words, couldn't stop yapping and laughing and asking questions as they made their way to the parking lot and his old truck.

"You still driving this heap?" asked Gil with a grin.

"Heap my butt! I rebuilt it from the ground up. Just get in, I'll show you."

They opted to take the back way to Prescott. After crawling through traffic, they cleared Sun City and picked up speed on the way to Wickenburg. There was lots to talk about. Not everything can be said in a letter, and this was guy talk.

"I batted 285 my last season in Australia."

"You did not."

"You know I don't lie! They let me be my own DH."

"Were all of them bunts for base hits?"

"Not all! I picked up one 12-6 curve and planted it in right field for a double last game of the season. But, yeah, the others were. Nothing wrong with that. They all know how fast I am, but when I get to the plate, all they see is a pitcher and figure I gotta be slow. I sure made believers of them. Even stole second a couple times."

And on it went. As they cruised through Congress with the truck purring happily, Tucker told Gil about becoming a dealer-certified mechanic for both Toyota and Ford.

"Well, doesn't surprise me. You always did excel in school."

"Shut up! Hell, when I first started, I didn't think I'd get past the first lesson. But after I saw how much more I could make, I became real motivated."

He said he was now working for a better shop and was their top mechanic. Things were going real well, and Gil just couldn't stop beaming at his buddy.

They left the Sonoran Desert and started up the winding 1800' climb, leading to the western edge of the Colorado Plateau. Partway up, Tucker fell silent. Gil thought he was concentrating on the tricky road, even though they had traversed it many times. But he was mistaken. As they neared the peak, Tucker shot him a look.

"You're still going to keep trying aren't you?"

"What kind of a dumb question is that? Have I reached the goal yet? No, I haven't. All these faraway places I've played don't mean nothing. You know what we're after. I got no choice but to keep going on. Hell, aren't you the one that told me never to quit?"

"Yeah. That was me. Just glad you haven't forgotten."

"Course I haven't forgotten! What's gotten into you?"

"Well, they haven't come out and said it, but Al and Mandy, are going to try and get you to hang it up. Stay in Prescott."

"Well, shoot, I sure hate to disappoint 'em! You know how women can be."

Tucker laughed heartily and punched the gas as they reached the top of Yarnell Hill. They motored along, gabbing all the way to Iron Springs Rd. As they cruised through Skull Valley, Tucker changed the topic.

"I ran into some of your dads awhile back. Jawbones blew a head gasket just down from the shop. Had to push his hog in. Satyr and Knuckles were with him. They were asking about you."

"I thought those two were in jail."

"Everybody's out by now, except Balrog, who apparently made more trouble when he was in the can and they tacked on time. After I fixed Jawbones' bike good, Diablo and Roadkill showed up with some work. Heard I was good. They all wanted to know where you were. I told 'em what I knew. They were real impressed. None of 'em are wearing patches anymore, nor flying the colors."

"Get out."

"They said most of 'em dropped the gang. Too much publicity. But they still have a clubhouse up in Chino. I guess they formed their own private group. Gave me the number to give to you." He popped his glovebox and pulled out a folded slip of paper.

"Thanks. Not sure if I really want to see them again."

"Understandable. But I figured it was my duty to let you decide."

Gil nodded and stuffed the slip in his wallet along with several other numbers and email addresses of scouts, players, host families, and former managers. He riffled through his savings money, saying, "By the way, I wanted to pay you back that money you lent me."

Tucker said, "So you're looking to get your arm broke again. Is that it?"

"Huh?"

"That was no loan! Someday you'll need it. You put that money back."

Gil could tell from Tucker's fixed jaw this was not a mere suggestion. He carefully folded his wallet and slipped it in his hip pocket.

As they started up the grade to Prescott, he said, "Sure is strange being back here."

Tucker chuckled. "I imagine it's going to get a whole lot stranger before it's over."

There was nothing too unusual or different about the town Gil remembered, except the new houses springing up everywhere. When they neared the apartment complex, his stomach tightened up. He wasn't sure what kind of reception he would receive. But Tucker drove right by the turnoff and continued toward downtown, saying he had to make a stop first.

They turned on Montezuma and drove past Whiskey Row. A few minutes later, they took Copper Basin Rd, then turned onto a small dead-end lane. Mature Ponderosa pines lined the way. Tucker stopped at the very last house and killed the engine.

It was the cutest little house, with a nice sized yard in front, and the rear bordering on a small woods. Gil imagined this would be the kind of place he'd like to get for Alice.

"I got a little business with the people here," said Tucker. "Come on, you'll like 'em."

Gil was not really in the mood, but he climbed out, nonetheless.

When they reached the front door, Tucker knocked, but got no response.

"Let's get on home. They must be away."

"Well, let's find out," said Tucker reaching for the door handle.

"Don't be doing that! This isn't your place!"

Tucker looked at him with a devilish grin. "Sure it is."

He whipped open the door and Gil saw a big banner reading, Welcome Home Gil, stretched across the top of the living room. Mandy popped up from behind the sofa, and Alice ran in from the hall, both screaming and clapping. Gil's mouth gaped. Everyone laughed at the sight. Mandy raced over and threw her arms around him. Gil locked eyes with Alice, and she smiled, all was forgiven.

His eyes caught sight of movement from under the coffee table. At first he thought it might be a dog, but then a little boy peeked his head out, eyes wide, staring at the unusual spectacle going on in his house. Gil's eyes widened as big as his as they stared at each other. Alice whispered in the boy's ear, then jabbed him lightly on the back. The toddler stumbled, then caught his balance and continued to Gil. He stared up, his face puckered in concentration.

"Welcome home, Uncle Gil."

Gil bit his lip, it was all too much in such a short time. His eyes started leaking tears as he stooped to the boy.

"You sad?" asked the boy.

Gil wiped his eyes. "No. What's your name?"

"Skip! But nana calls me Skipper."

Gil looked at Alice. "Aw, mom!"

"It was just a suggestion!"

He swung his head to Tucker. "Tuckeroo, you didn't."

"Hey! I can't help it if Mandy's crazy for Gilligan's Island too. What was I gonna do, call him Ginger?" Everyone laughed except Skip who grabbed Gil's shirt to get his attention back where it belonged.

"You play baseball?"

"Sure do."

"You teach me?"

Gil stared into his eyes. "You know I will."

Skip howled with glee as he raced to the sofa and started tearing around on it, bouncing up and down and doing half flips. Mandy rushed over before he broke his neck, and scooped him up.

"I wanted to tell you, Gil," she said hurriedly. "But Tuck didn't want me to. Said it would distract you. Take your mind off your playing."

"And he was probably right. I guess I missed out on a lot of things, from the looks of it." He jutted his chin at the ring on Tucker's hand.

Tucker blushed. "Yeah. We're hitched. But it wasn't a big deal. We just went down to the courthouse, saw a JP."

"Oh. Congratulations."

"I told you we should have let him know!" cried Mandy. "He said he wouldn't miss it for the world!"

"We already talked about that!" said Tucker. "Gil, we were thinking once you got back we could kind of do a replay. You know, have a proper wedding so you can be a part of it. Hell, I didn't even have a best man when we did it the first time."

Gil smiled and shook his head. "We'll do nothing of the kind. It's silly to spend all that money just for me. I'm just tickled you two are tied together for good now. And you got a family, like it should be. And a real nice house. How'd you manage that?"

"Well, it's not exactly all ours yet. It's a rent to own. We didn't have the down payment, but in a couple years, once that's covered, we'll get our very own mortgage and be owing until I'm I'll old and gray. The American Dream, right buddy?"

"You said it. Fact is, I'm hoping to get a place like this for mom. Can't stand her being in that apartment for another minute."

Alice stepped up and laid a hand on his arm. "I live here with them, honey."

"What?"

"It made sense, Gil. Couldn't have done it without all three of us paying rent."

"And it's a perfect setup for all of us!" added Mandy. "I'm a bank teller, so Al takes care of Skip during the day until I get home. Then she goes into the restaurant."

Gil had never felt such a mix of emotions. He could do nothing but look back and forth from one to the other.

Tucker, voice shaking, said, "I wasn't trying to get in your way. I know you had plans for Al. It's just, well, like she said, it made a lot of sense. You understand?"

Gil nodded, realizing he had long ago given up his right to interfere. His was a solitary path, and people can't be expected to stop living their lives because of him. He abruptly grabbed Tucker in a bear hug.

"You once said I was your hero. Well, now you're mine Tuck."

When he broke the embrace, he turned and there was Alice, tears streaming. He opened his arms and she melted into him. The charged atmosphere dissipated and there was a collective sigh of relief.

Dinner that night was a festive occasion. The ladies pulled out all the stops and provided a spread fit for a returning knight. The chatter was nonstop, with everyone getting to know each other again. Gil watched as his mom doted on Skip, seeing how much it meant to her being part of this family. She had a new child to look after, and no longer needed to fret over him. He was not sad over this, for Alice looked so happy she was literally glowing.

After dinner, he regaled everyone with funny stories from his adventures in far flung places. They listened in awe, hardly believing what he had seen and done. Gil was taken aback by their amazement. It was only then it dawned on him how much he had indeed changed, and how far he had come. He didn't exactly feel out of place, just different, and antsy.

That night, he was shown to the third bedroom, as yet, unoccupied, just waiting for him. He was informed that Skip slept in Tucker and Mandy's room.

All his familiar baseball posters and memorabilia were hung on the walls, everything laid out just like when he was a kid. But as he lay there trying to find sleep, he wondered why he felt like he was in a stranger's room.

Chapter 15

IT DIDN'T TAKE LONG FOR GIL TO FEEL COMFORTABLE with everyone going out of their way to make sure he was. After the initial celebration, things returned to a normal routine, everyone going off to their jobs, meals being fixed, chores taken care of. He spent the days hanging with Alice and Skip. The boy took to him instantly, and soon they were tossing around a nerf ball and playing mock baseball games.

In the evenings, after Alice went to work, Gil prepared dinner for the rest of them, using the new dishes he'd learned. One afternoon, Alice said she wanted him to see her new restaurant. They drove over and Gil was impressed. It was the fanciest place she'd served tables, and she made a big deal of showing him off to her fellow workers. She made a specific point of introducing him to the head chef, and touting Gil as quite the budding cook. Partway through, he realized what was going on. The chef asked questions like in an interview. Later, he met the manager, and again, it felt like a setup.

There were other things. When Gil would talk about playing ball overseas, Alice would smile, and then say something like, "What an accomplishment. Not many people can say they did what you did. I'd call that success."

Gil translated it as, "You've already reached your goal. There's no point wasting anymore time trying to go further." He knew she wasn't being mean. It's just she didn't want him going away again. Perhaps, when he was young and she was in on the dream, she didn't quite realize what sacrifices it would take—from everybody.

Mandy also made no secret of her feelings. She made a regular point of saying how happy Tucker was now that his best friend was home. And how much Skip loved playing with his uncle. At dinner it was, "Gil, how did we ever survive this long without you in the kitchen?" Stuff like that. Gil was glad he had been forewarned by Tucker, or he might not have seen it for what it was and be lulled into the security of a normal life.

A week after he arrived, his birthday party took place. It was just the family, but there was a cake with ice cream, party hats and noisemakers. Skip presented Gil with a crayon drawing of the two of them, hand in hand, a bright yellow sun smiling down. Gil made a big production of hanging it on the refrigerator in a place of honor.

Next came Mandy and Alice's gift, and Gil had to do a little playacting to pretend how excited he was when it turned out to be a dreaded phone. It was, thankfully, not too fancy, and the type where you add minutes online when you need them, with no formal contract or regular monthly fee. But it was a smartphone, and after an hour of the ladies trying to show him all the features, he felt dumber than ever.

When it came Tucker's turn, it appeared he had kept his gift secret from everyone, much to Mandy's frustration. She told him he needed to get it from its hiding spot. With a grin, he said he couldn't do that. There was no package. She and Alice began to scold him when he backed them down and led Gil to the computer.

"Type in your name." Gil wanted to know why, and Tucker said, Shut up and do it."

He did, and a panel popped up on the right side of the screen with his name, an old picture, and a short description stating he was a switch-pitcher. Gil stared at it, not believing his eyes. Alice and Mandy were equally dumbfounded.

"You're on Wikipedia, brother," said Tucker.

"I thought that was for famous people," said Gil.

"Nope. You just have to have done something notable. I tried posting it when you first played for the state leagues in Australia, but they nixed it. It's when you were with the ABL they finally approved it. You're a cinch. They'll never take it down. I sure could use a new picture, though. This is from high school. You still got pimples."

"I can't believe this," said Alice, trying unsuccessfully to hide her disapproval.

"Oh, it gets better," said Tucker, ignoring her attitude. "Type in switch-pitcher."

"Look, it's Venditte, he's pitching great lately. And here's an article about Harris."

"I know. I haven't figured out how to get higher up in the search results. Scroll down." He pointed at a link for the website, *switchpitcher.com*.

Gil clicked on it and a page popped up. Across the top was a bold banner, reading, "G-MAN! BASEBALL'S NEXT GREAT SWITCH-PITCHER."

"I have my own website?"

"More like a webpage. I don't have all the info I need to flush it out. Hoping you could catch me up so I can fill out all the details. Keep your fans up-to-date."

Alice and Mandy locked eyes, both knowing this was not helping their cause.

"How much did all this cost?" asked Mandy, testily.

"None of your business. This is my gift to Gil. Hope you like it buddy. I tried getting you on baseball-reference, but you have to have been in the majors at least once. I expect that's coming soon."

Gil's eyes sparkled. "Real soon."

"Alright then, we'll let the ladies clean up, while you bring me up to speed with all your stats. And I don't want your encyclopedic brain to leave anything out. We'll post them right now. Then we'll get a couple of pictures. Sound good to you girls?"

Alice and Mandy were in a spot. They wanted to argue, tell him not to encourage Gil, but they both knew it was a losing proposition. They pasted on half-smiles and, harrumphing in unison, retired to the kitchen.

Into the night, Gil and Tucker worked on the web pages. At Tucker's suggestion, Gil sent emails to past managers and host families requesting photos. Noah enthusiastically sent on a batch of real good ones. Gil told him and his other contacts if they ever needed to send a message they could do it through the website. He also grudgingly passed on his new number.

As they looked at their newly designed pages, Tucker said, "You know I wasn't kidding. You really do have fans. I get messages from people everywhere you've played, even the Czechs. And after you kicked butt in the Caribbean Series, I expect I'll hear from people down there."

"It's hard to believe, but I sure appreciate their support. I'll bet a lot of them have some good pictures of me playing."

"Shoot. Why didn't I think of that? I'll put up a notice on the homepage saying we're looking for any fan photos. I'll bet we get a bunch."

"I don't know how to thank you, Tuck."

"You know what I want. And you'll get there. Did I tell you Chip Benson got drafted?

They picked him up right after graduation. He's somewhere in the Padres system. I think he's playing Class A ball down in Fort Wayne."

"The TinCaps. Good for him. He deserves it. What happened to Jimmy Reese?"

"The Nationals drafted him out of college his sophomore year, but he blew his arm out in Double A. Had to have surgery. I'm not sure if he's healed up yet or not."

"Damn shame. Should've stuck to the slider rather than always throwing heat."

They were silent for a time, until Tucker said, "When's the next tryout?"

"Soon."

"I figured."

"First one's in Tucson. Then onto wherever else I gotta go. If nothing happens, I'm back overseas. No way I can stop playing now. I'm just getting good."

Tucker belly laughed. After a pause, he said, "How you gonna tell Al?"

"I was thinking a letter. I hate goodbyes."

"Suit yourself, but you better tell me before you go. I'm not as forgiving."

Gil smiled. A text came through on Tucker's phone and he checked it, grinned, and sent back a reply. Gil thought nothing of it. But a minute later his phone rang.

"Who could that be? Nobody knows this number except the people I just sent it to."

"Well, I may have dropped it to one or two others," said Tucker stifling a giggle.

Gil frowned and answered. "Hello? Danny! Boy it's been a long time!—Huh? Well, I'm sorry. Yeah, I know I had your number but I figured you being a college boy your time was all used up with books, and girls, and more girls—Alright, I apologize! Huh? That would take a long time—okay, okay, hold on."

He looked at Tucker who grinned and motioned that he was going to bed. He slapped Gil on the back and headed for his room.

Gil went back to the phone. "Alright, I'll start at the beginning, after Cooperstown."

It was closing on midnight before the two had sufficiently caught up—including Gil's news he was no longer a virgin. Danny was soon to graduate and expected to move on to law school—something he was not too keen on. He said he didn't realize how much he would miss baseball.

When they finally hung up, Gil felt that familiar feeling in his gut. It was time to move on. Danny had been impressed with how much he had achieved, but still appalled no MLB team had seen the light. He urged Gil to keep fighting the good fight.

He sat alone for a while, making his plans. A thought came to him and he pulled out a slip of paper from his contacts. He dialed the number and waited.

"Jawbones there? Tell him it's G-Man. Hey, Jawbones, it's me. Yeah, I'm alright. I'll catch you up when I see you. No not tonight. Thing is I need a favor from you and one of the other boys."

The next day, he borrowed Alice's car, saying he wanted to visit some old haunts. In truth, he went to the Walmart and purchased two prepaid credit cards. He then went to a sporting goods store and bought new cleats, his old ones were pretty shot.

The next few days passed swiftly. At times, he caught Alice giving him sidelong glances, like she knew what was in his head. Tucker was also watching him closely.

One day, Gil presented Skip with a toddler's T-Ball set. He went gaga over it, whacking the ball all over the living room, and causing all kinds of havoc until Alice insisted it was an outdoor toy. They promptly moved to the yard.

It was Alice's night off, and Gil prepared Pollo Guisado, a specialty he learned from Mama Fuentes in the Dominican Republic. Everyone raved over it. After dinner, Skip showed off his batting skills to his dad, and then headed to bed. The adults spread out in the living room, pretending to be watching the TV. But everyone was surreptitiously eyeing Gil, sensing something was up. He sat on the edge of the sofa, left foot bouncing nervously, like waiting for a cue.

It came at nine, on the dot. A terrific rumble filled the air outside and he shot to his feet and departed to his room. He quickly returned with his small suitcase and holding two envelopes, which he placed on the coffee table.

Facing the others, he said, "I have to go. Right now. And I'm no good at this. But I didn't want to slip away like a thief in the dark like last time."

Tucker started to say something, but Gil butted in. "I already have a ride, buddy. Two of the boys are going to take me down south tonight. Don't argue! You have work tomorrow. And you've done so much for me already. Same with you, Mandy. Thanks for making things so nice, and welcoming me to your home."

"It's your home too, Gil!" cried Mandy.

"Not for now. And mom I sure wish I could be what you want me to be. But I can't work in no restaurant. I hope you'll at least wish me luck."

Alice slowly stood and walked to him, placing her hands on his shoulders. "You're exactly who you're meant to be, Gil. And you don't need any luck from me. I can't hope to understand what drives you on, but it's all you're going to need. You're too stubborn not to win at this game. And I'm so proud of you I can't put it into words."

She pulled him in tight, then he broke the embrace, saying, "The boys are waiting. You tell the little one I'm gonna miss him something awful. And tell him to keep practicing. He's got a good swing."

He grabbed his suitcase and headed for the door. Partway out, he turned. "I have a few other things I want to say, but I figured I'd do better in a letter. It's in the top envelope. Open that one first. Alright then. You take care now."

And out into the night he went. There was a fleet of five hogs waiting for him. All driven by his dads. Only one missing was Balrog. Gil jogged up to Jawbones and said, "I told you I only needed two of you. One for me and one for the bag."

Jawbones eyed the grown-up Gil with pride. "Once I told them it was you, I couldn't fight 'em off if I tried. Hop on. You've got a full escort tonight." He looked over Gil's shoulders and his eyes widened when he saw Alice approaching. "Hey, Al. Lookin' mighty fine."

"Watch your mouth!" barked Alice. "And you better get my boy safely where he's going. Anything happens to him and you'll answer to me. That goes for all of you!"

"Yes, ma'am," mumbled the hardened bikers, like answering an angry schoolmarm.

"Now get!" ordered Alice.

In procession, the bikes wheeled around and motored down the short drive, disappearing into the night. Alice turned and found Tucker and Mandy looking at her. They hooked arms and walked slowly into the house.

They eased themselves onto the sofa, and Tucker lifted the first envelope. He slit it open and pulled out a single sheet of paper.

"Dear family," he read. "I'll keep this short and sweet because I only have a couple of things to say. I wish I could have been a part of getting this sweet house, but that time is past. However, I hope to relieve a little bit of the burden by offering the only thing I can give, which is in the other envelope."

Tucker handed the second envelope to Mandy. "It's not a lot, but I hope it allows you to cover the down payment quicker on this place and get you out of paying rent."

"Tuck!" said Mandy excitedly. "There's got to be ten thousand dollars in here!"

"You sure?!"

"I work in a bank, silly. I think I can count money!"

She handed the envelope to Alice, and Tucker continued reading. "I still have plenty to get by on, and so far people are willing to pay my way as long as I can play. Second thing, and this is important, starting tomorrow, I want you to give my room to Skip. When I come to visit I can sleep on the couch. But that boy needs a room of his own. I hope you will not hesitate in fulfilling this request. I love you all. Gil. P.S. I left something in the room so Skip won't forget who his uncle is."

Tucker's shoulders heaved, and Alice laid a hand on his back. He shot to his feet and walked down the hall to Gil's room. His eyes landed above the bed. Hanging on the wall was one of the Korean pennants with *G-Man* printed in shiny gold lettering.

Top of the 6th

EVER SINCE I LEFT PRESCOTT, for two solid years, I've had something stuck in my brain I can't shake. Through all the unsuccessful tryouts in the States, playing in Europe again, first for Greece and last summer for Austria, and yet another two seasons in the ABL and KBO, it's never left, like a dumb song in your head you can't seem to shed.

I'm awful afraid this nagging problem is going to hurt my pitching. So I decided to use this journal to write out my thoughts in hopes I can solve the mystery. I have a feeling other people who choose to set off on a journey like mine will face it as well. Maybe if I can figure it out, it will help others down the road.

It started when my mom said she couldn't understand what it was that keeps me chasing this dream. I didn't think much of it, because I felt sure I knew the answer. But later I realized I had never thought that deep about it.

As a kid, I was doing it for her, to get her a better life. But now she's got a house and a family to keep her happy. So why do I go on? If not for her, then who? Me? Do I really desire fame and money so much? I can't believe that's true. It's not in my nature.

Maybe the dream itself is its own force. At first it was something a little kid imagined, then it became real and powerful. A living thing. And now I'm just a slave working for it. And it'll keep consuming me until it comes true, or eats me alive.

Or maybe it's my talent I'm a slave to. There's no denying I'm good. And when someone knows that about themselves they must surrender to it and live by its rules. What else can you do? Squander it? You can't. You have to fight to show it. But for who's benefit? If you already know you're talented what's the point in proving it?

The easier way to look at it is to believe a higher power has given me a task and I have no choice but to carry it out. Well, that might work for some, but I never was a believer. And even if there was such a thing, it's unlikely I'd be their Chosen One.

I've talked to players who are stuck in the same situation. Traveling all over the damn world, getting paid peanuts, just to follow a dream. Some say they're doing it for the love of the game. It sure is easy rolling off the tongue. But something always gets stuck in my throat. Of course I love the game! Hell, if that's all it was, I could've stayed in Prescott and played in a beer league.

There's something more. I believe it does involve my love for the game, but in a deeper way. It really comes down to deciding to be a switch-pitcher. It would have been a whole lot easier if I'd just chosen to be normal. Because that's what's killing me in the tryouts. Noah talked about it in Cooperstown, but I didn't listen. Americans think they're responsible for upholding the tradition of the game. And except for a few oddballs like me, there is no tradition of switch-pitchers.

So why do I do it? Is it just that I'm stubborn, like mom says? Of course she's right, but lately I think I'm sticking to my guns for another reason. I've always believed the game of baseball must adapt to the players, like the players adapt to the game. Because no game is just a set of rules. It's made up of people, with all kinds of skills. When Nolan Ryan started throwing over 100 mph, the players had to adapt, but so did the game.

I think even as a kid I realized it only took one player to change the way the game was played, to push the boundaries, make it more interesting, better. And I truly believe the game would be better with switch-pitchers. I think the sport has an obligation to move beyond what was and stretch itself to the limits. Rather than shun, it should embrace any player who has the ability and guts to challenge tradition. Every generation has had one of those players. And I feel it's my duty to be the one for mine. Even if it kills me. That's how much I love this game. And that's what drives me on.

At least that's what I'm going to tell myself from now on. One thing that's nice about being human, you'll never know if you're right, but it's real easy to believe you are. With that in mind, I'll settle on this as the answer and wipe my mind clean before this question drives me insane.

I'm over the damn ocean again. I've given up trying to know which one, so I just think of it as one body of water. And every time I see it, up here in the sky, it seems to have grown bigger and bigger, like it's working to swallow up everything in its path.

Chapter 16

FOR THE FIRST TIME SINCE GIL LEFT HOME he was playing ball in his own country. It wasn't the sort of team he imagined he'd be with when he first set out, but at least he was on familiar ground. And most everybody spoke English. The Revolution, or Revs, was a member of the Freedom division of the Atlantic League.

By now, he was well-known internationally, and had several offers to play overseas this summer. But he opted to pitch for far less money in the historic town of York, Pennsylvania. It was due to the fact the Atlantic League had unofficially become a proving ground of potential recruits for the big leagues. Out of the myriad Independent Leagues, this one offered the best chance to reach the show through the back door.

He was twenty-five, four years since last visiting his family, eight years playing year-round ball. He would not admit it, but when he looked in the mirror, he saw the hungry look he had seen so many years ago on players who were afraid their time was up. He did an admirable job of hiding his feelings, but, at times, played with a level of abandon that was frightful.

As usual, he was a fan favorite. Before games, he entertained the crowd with his juggling skills. He spent an hour before and after games signing autographs and talking with children, naively eager to follow in his footsteps.

He was equally beloved by his teammates. Days off, he cooked meals for the guys at his host family's house. This was most appreciated due to the small meal allowance given the players, and the 10% clubhouse dues deducted from their meager salaries. On bus rides to away games, he would regale them with his knowledge of physics and its importance to baseball. During games, he was a prankster in the dugout, always cheering everyone up, despite the score.

The Atlantic League was not only a testing ground for new players. In recent years, the MLB had been proposing new rules—many designed to shorten the duration of games. The Atlantic League had become the place to try them out without prematurely shaking the foundation of the big leagues. They were like the petri dish for professional baseball. Some of the rules would never be adopted, but one being tried out was the reason Gil had been hired by the Revolution.

Changing pitchers midgame is time-consuming, therefore, the idea was to require pitchers to face a minimum of three batters. If the rule was ever put into place in the majors, it would cause all kinds of turmoil. Relief pitchers are specialists, trained to attack specific batters, and often replaced after one at-bat. To adjust to the rule, they would need to be trained differently. It was indeed a game changer. Unless, of course, a team had a switch-pitcher on their roster—like the Revs had in Gil.

And so when the signal came to the bullpen in the top of the seventh during a midseason home game against the

Lancaster Barnstormers, Gil knew exactly what his job was. There was already one out, but the Barnstormers had the bases loaded, and the score was tied. Gil needed to get the next two men to prevent a run, then follow through into the top of the eighth for at least one more batter.

"How you feeling?" asked the manager as they huddled on the mound.

"About falling asleep until now. Sure gets hot and sticky in these parts."

"They tell me that's what makes the corn grow so good."

"Is that a fact? Then I'll stop griping. Nothing better than an ear of sweet corn."

"Sit these two guys down, I'll buy you a bushel of Silver Queen."

"Done."

The manager left for the dugout and Gil played a little toss with his catcher. Pitchers were allowed eight warmup pitches, but Gil never used them. He felt it was a waste of bullets, and he didn't like showing his stuff to upcoming batters. After a few lobs with his left arm, he switched his glove to toss a few with his right. That's when the crowd really started buzzing. This is what they had come to see.

There was one person, however, who was seeing him for the first time. It was the reason he was here. At the urging of an associate, he tried to see him pitch years ago while he was in high school. But Gil never got the ball that game. Now, he had the opportunity to see the player of whom he had heard many rumors ever since.

His name was Jaxon "JJ" Jaggard. He was in his 60's and known as a man who could recognize talent in a sea of wannabees. He had been a pitcher in the minors, but injuries derailed his career. Since then, he made his haphazard living as a bird dog scout. He loved his job.

There was nothing better than finding an overlooked gem amongst the worthless scree. His search led him far and wide: community colleges, Independent Leagues, beer leagues, even junior high schools.

As an independent bird dog, he did not have the power to sign a player, but if he discovered real talent he contacted a scout higher up the ladder who could make a deal. Most never questioned his word and looked forward to his calls.

The first batter strode quickly to the plate. Gil saw he was young, anxious to make a name for himself. What better way than to hit a grand slam? He was a lefty, and Gil therefore pitched right. He watched the batter look to his dugout for instructions. Gil didn't need to know the signs. The situation was obvious. The batter was told to bunt for a squeeze. Gil was looking for his reaction. When he saw the slight pout appear, he knew the player was disappointed, and was about to disobey his manager. He would intentionally blow the first two bunt attempts, leaving no option but to swing away. The information made Gil's job a lot easier.

The first two pitches were purposefully high and wide and the player foolishly offered the bunt on both. Two strikes. It was simple enough now to play into the batter's intentions. The catcher was also in sync with Gil's thinking, and called for a curve. The batter swung well before the 72-mph ball reached the plate. Two outs.

Gil knew the next batter. A seasoned player, up and down from the minors to the majors, but never able to make it stick in the big time. He was still, however, a genuine threat. He was a righty, so Gil switched to pitch left. The crowd went wild, loving this odd twist to the age-old game.

Gil started out with two sinkers, both nipped for foul balls. His third was a slow four-seam fastball—a dangerous choice given the speed, but it came in high, and the experienced batter spit at it. The catcher called for another, thinking it would be unexpected, but Gil shook him off. They settled on an inside slider.

Gil knew it had to be perfect, unhittable, but tempting enough to swing. The ball started out wide, then corrected course and headed into the plate. Sensing an error in delivery, the old pro started to swing. But during the last fifteen feet, the ball dipped down, sweeping inside to his back ankle. A Randy Johnson Special. The bat met air, and the inning was over.

A familiar feeling stirred in JJ's gut. Hayes was a diamond in the rough.

The bottom of the seventh saw an early out, but the second batter was plunked by a pitch. The third man moved him over with a line drive single to left field. Gil was up, and the manager grabbed him.

"No heroics, Gil. Just move him over."

"Heck, Coach. I'm no Flash."

"Yeah, right. Seriously. I need your arms, not the base."

Gil shrugged and walked to the plate. Normally, he always did what his manager told him, and he had no intention to do otherwise. But he had noticed the opposing pitcher did not field his position well. He was nervous when the ball came his way, and had a clumsy throw to first. It was just a passing thought, but one he could not erase. When the first pitch came in, he let it pass. It was a high strike, and he was too accomplished a bunter to fall for that.

The second pitch, however, was a mistake, and he jumped on it. It seemed a near perfect bunt, rolling down the inside of the first base line. As he bolted from the plate, however, he noticed it had been hit a little too hard. The pitcher would get to it a step too early. But even as he sped along, he knew he had done his job. There was no way to stop the base runners from moving over. He should take the out and call it good.

But just up ahead was first base. A few more yards and he would be in reach. That's when raw instinct took over—and reason foolishly cast aside. There is never a good time to slide headfirst into first. The only situation where maybe it is acceptable was this very moment. It would give the pitcher nothing to tag. He heard heavy breathing bearing down. He imagined the pitcher reaching out, striving for a swipe.

He dove, helmet flying off, body skimming just above the dirt like a plane coming in for a landing. Arms outstretched, his fingers sought purchase, eyes sighting the white, upraised goal only inches ahead. He felt the hard rubber. He was there—safe.

At exactly the same moment, a shadow appeared, crushing down, cleats obscuring taut fingers. A blinding light flashed, blocking all thought. As the pain rushed over him, his body instinctively curled and he rolled over and over, clutching his right hand. A din filled his ears as the crowd roared in horror.

JJ jerked his eyes from the terrible sight. As the manager and players poured out of the dugout, he looked to his notebook and scratched out Gil's name, shaking his head over the loss of what might have been. He stood up to go. In his gut, he knew the kid had the right stuff, but there was nothing more to be seen here.

Chapter 17

TUCKER HAD GONE FROM IRRITATED, to frustrated, to angry, and finally, desperately worried. Five months he and Gil had been out of contact. After the last visit to Prescott they had done a good job of staying in touch. They often talked on the phone, where Gil updated him with statistics and achievements from wherever he was playing. Tucker had become his PR man. Maintaining the website, answering posts from fans, starting a Facebook page, and giving Gil an online presence.

Gil often sent on packages containing gifts, and money. Tucker wondered how his pal managed to stay alive what with sending on most of his earnings. Gil would say it should be used for the family's needs, but with the exception of his original donation toward the down payment, the monies were promptly placed in a savings account, never to be touched until his return.

Even though Gil was always far away, Tucker felt he was just around the corner. Now he was gone. He first heard of the injury from a Revolution fan. He immediately contacted the manager who said Gil had simply disappeared after the fateful game.

He began calling Gil's phone. After two months with no response, he got a recording informing him the service had lapsed. He posted a request on the website, asking for any sightings. He even put the word out to the boys, knowing their connections to other biker clubs spanned the globe. All to no avail. He tried hiding this from Alice, but she caught on, and was now in a terrible state. She was either snapping at the slightest thing, or buried in depression with only silence to keep her company.

The family had been used to periods of time without contact, but always knowing he was there in spirit. Now it was different, and eerily strange. Like someone was presumed dead, but without proof, the living must continue on with nothing but invisible strands of hope. A soldier missing in action.

It was the questioning eyes that were getting to Tucker, from Mandy and Alice, but especially Skip, who now idolized his uncle. Eyes always boring into him, hungry for information, but afraid to ask. With nothing to give, he'd see the flicker of expectation fizzle and die, only to be reborn the next morning.

Privately, he wondered if he was to blame. He had never made it a secret to Gil that their dream was one and the same. He could not imagine life without the ever-present knowledge he was connected to someone who dared to live beyond the norm. A rare bird. But who was he to put such pressure on the one expected to succeed? If—no, when he found Gil he would let him know that in his mind he had won the game long ago, simply by attempting the inconceivable.

Danny had officially decided he'd gotten all he needed from the law. After struggling through law school, he managed to graduate in three years and attain his Juris

Doctor Degree. Passing the bar was a whole other story. He tried three times, and failed. This caused great embarrassment to his father, but, as usual, Danny could care less.

He knew his path lay elsewhere. In school, the one area in which he excelled was contract law. He was a natural bargainer and liked the satisfaction of getting a good deal for his client. His first experience in doing so was back in Cooperstown when he had negotiated with Noah on Gil's behalf. It was a little thing, but it stuck with him. And it's what drove him to finally give up the thought of being a lawyer and go back to sports.

With his family's connections, he landed a position as a junior agent under the mentorship of Abe Scally, one of the top sports agents in the country. He began working for him in June, just a year after leaving law school. He quickly learned the ropes, and worked diligently managing many of his accounts. Abe told him, however, the only way he would become a full-fledged agent was to recruit players of his own. The agency handled all sports, but because of his background, Danny was relegated to baseball.

The first man to come to mind was Gil. He reached out to him, but drew a blank. He contacted Tucker and found out about the injury and the ensuing disappearance of their champion. At first, it didn't worry him, believing Gil would eventually surface, good as new. But months passed, and still no word. He managed to sign a couple of power hitters straight out of college, which temporarily appeased Abe, but he was still looking for that one player who he believed in with all his heart. The one he would lift from obscurity to the big time. The one who had inadvertently led him to his life's work.

But it was more than just his feelings about Gil that made him the perfect candidate. Baseball was changing. Old conventions being tested and broken. Instinctively, Danny knew the time was ripe for a switch-pitcher. And as far as he could tell, there was only one out there who could tackle the big leagues and come out on top.

Using the resources available through his father's law offices, he began a methodical search. So far, months had passed and nothing turned up. Winter was coming on. A new season was on the horizon. The clock was ticking.

Oliver "Ollie" Denning had not wasted any time leaving Prescott High School. After his rift with Coach Reynolds, he gave notice. He landed a job as a trainer with ASU, and over four years rose to top pitching coach for the acclaimed Division I team.

His success led to his recruitment by the Arizona Diamondbacks. He started in Class A, coaching for the Kane County Cougars, but moved swiftly into Double-A with the Jackson Generals. The front office was so impressed, he was promoted and for the past two years was in charge of the pitching squad for the franchise's Triple-A team in Reno, NV. The Aces, a perennial powerhouse, were part of the highly competitive Pacific Coast League.

In June, he received a call from his long-term associate, JJ Jaggard. The scout said he was finally going to see the player that Ollie had touted years ago in Prescott. Ollie was enthusiastic. He had never gotten Gil out of his mind, and had followed his career on his website. He was happy Gil was playing ball, but felt he was meant for more than the international and independent leagues. Perhaps this was his chance to break through. So when the follow-up call came, with JJ describing the terrible accident, Ollie was appalled—even more so upon hearing Jaggard's prediction that Gil's serious injury would likely sideline him forever.

Ollie contacted Tucker through the website and found that Gil had gone underground. It was a natural response, and he had seen it many times before with injured players. For a time, Gil was forced from his mind. There was a season to play.

It was only during a recent post-season meeting that again the name, G-Man, formed silently on his lips. The Aces manager was already getting his coaches prepared for the upcoming season. It was revealed the MLB was indeed going to adopt some of the rule changes recently tested in the Atlantic League.

The one that demanded the most attention was the rule requiring every pitcher to face a minimum of three batters. The Aces manager let Denning know the Diamondbacks would be seriously looking into their farm teams for pitchers who could live up to the requirement. Extra pre-season training would be essential. A change in approach, and attitude, was imperative.

Ollie sat quietly, recognizing the difficulties the new rule would bring. His brain scanned the known pitchers who would be returning to his squad. And it was then, unbidden, Gil's name had arisen. He could not bring it up in the meeting. He had no power to suggest possible acquisitions. Even if he had, he would have been laughed out of the room at the suggestion. But he could not shake the feeling a solution was at hand. What better weapon to combat the new rule than a switch-pitcher?

He had seen many pitchers come and go over the years, but not one came close to possessing the kind of heart needed to topple the pillars of tradition. In short, if there was ever a time Gil was needed, it was now.

Chapter 18

WHEN THE CLEATS LANDED ON GIL'S HAND it was more than bones that broke. The real disaster occurred within his mind. His spirit was shattered. The dogged will to fight against all odds, and achieve his goal no matter what, was seemingly beyond repair. He had been on the edge for more than a year, wondering if he had chosen the wrong path. He saw the accident as a clear message. The journey was over.

He was quiet as the trainer rushed him to the locker room and did a cursory examination. His index and middle finger was where the main injury occurred, and he watched as they were taped together to prevent bending. It was unclear if they were broken or dislocated. They would have to see what the X-rays showed the following day. Gil waited until he was alone, then calmly gathered his gear and walked the two blocks to his host family's house. He was grateful no one was home as he packed his suitcase. He could not write a letter thanking them—as he always did for his hosts— because he never learned to write with his left hand.

He walked back to the ballpark, stopping just outside the Greyhound Bus Station abutting the stadium. He could hear the crowd cheering, and slipped inside the terminal to shut out the beloved sounds he could no longer bear to hear. He bought a ticket bound for Phoenix. He wasn't sure it was his ultimate destination, but he could think of no other place to tell the cashier. He opted for a flexible fare, allowing changes to his travel plans en route. The trip was estimated at 57 hours and 20 minutes. It took him three months to finally reach his home state.

His first transfer was in Indianapolis and by then the swelling and throbbing was so severe he left the station and found a fleabag motel. The next day, he sought out a clinic and waited four hours to see a doctor. After the accident, he hadn't even considered if the Revolution carried insurance on their players. He was not about to make the team suffer over his mistake.

When he explained how the injury occurred, the doctor immediately suggested he go to an emergency room, but he refused. He politely told him if there was nothing he could do, the fingers would remain as they were. Against his better judgement, but driven by his sworn duty to heal—and his love of baseball players—the doctor proceeded to set the index finger which had been broken. He also did his best to relocate the middle finger that was dislocated. He warned Gil surgery might be required. Splints were applied, and he was sent on his way.

He returned to his motel and spent the next month in a daze, staring at the walls, replaying the accident over and over. When he couldn't stand it any longer, he got back on a bus, and continued his trip. It had been awhile since he sent money home, so he had a little over $2000 after the bus ticket and the medical costs. He also had the emergency poker stake in his wallet, which he hoped not to have to touch.

The bus route cut straight through the heartland of the country, endless fields with nothing to break the monotony, only time to think. Gil had never experienced true depression, and it hit him hard. He had always had a plan, a destination, a goal. Now he had nothing. His inner thoughts were dullish, repetitive, and unfamiliar, like he had lost touch with his mind. By the time the terrain turned to desert, he was going stir-crazy.

At a quick stop in Tucumcari, New Mexico, he frantically stumbled outside, breaking free of the moving prison, and began to walk. He found a bargain motel, and could go no farther. That night, his stomach ached. He was hungrier than he had ever been, but when he wandered the aisles of a nearby convenience store the only thing that drew him was a case of cheap beer.

He lugged it back to his room, hoping this might be the cure, the thing that would keep at bay the creeping blackness threatening to swallow him whole. For a week, and several spent cases of beer, it worked. Then his body, unused to alcohol, revolted. It took him the better part of another week to fully recover.

Though no one had been privy to his transgression, he was disgusted with himself. Never one to wallow in self-pity or booze, he wasn't about to start now. He must fully embrace his new reality and move on. To do so, he would have to reprogram his brain. No more thinking of what might have been or what he should have done. He would move forward. Find a new path.

He thought of calling Tucker. He always felt better after talking things out. But for now he didn't have that option. In his drunken fog he had discovered fifty-two unanswered messages on his phone—most from Tucker, but there were others who were looking for him. At the time, however, he was too inebriated and angry at the world to respond. Instead, he deleted all of them without listening and threw the phone into a dumpster. He wished he hadn't and was thinking about getting a new one, but money was getting tight. It would have to wait. He decided this wasn't such a bad thing. There would be time enough to talk to people once he had reconfigured himself into something more presentable.

He spent a long time wondering who it was he should be now that his dream was over. His inspiration came from Tucker. He had done well for himself, with a good job, a home, and family. These were not things Gil had ever desired, but they were honorable pursuits. And what was good enough for his best friend, was good enough for him. Convinced of his new path, the first thing to do was get a job.

He had no skills other than baseball and cooking, and the latter would require the use of his right hand. The doctor said it was important not to delay the start of rehabilitation, and he was already overdue, it being now nearly ten weeks since the accident. One night, with shaking hands, he removed the splints. His two injured fingers looked relatively normal, but when he tried to move them they were stiff and painful.

Little by little, he began the slow process of bringing them back to life. After a week, he gained movement, but noticed his middle finger seemed to be stuck in a permanent bend. His index finger also curled inward slightly at the top joint. If there had ever been any doubt, this cinched it. Be it from scar tissue or ruptured ligaments, his fingers were forever disfigured, and his pitching days were over. He'd known it since the moment it happened, but was still overcome and had to choke back the grief.

His stubborn constitution fought back, and he began scouring the small city of Tucumcari, seeking out a position in one of the few restaurants. He had worked in several eateries during off-seasons, but only for short stints and always in foreign lands. This did not sit well with the places he applied. It didn't take him long to realize he must continue his search elsewhere.

Returning to Prescott was not an option, not until he had something to show for himself. But Arizona's familiar surroundings kept calling. It was time to go home.

The night before his bus arrived, he packed his few belongings. There were things he no longer needed to lug around and he didn't hesitate in disposing of them. Into the dumpster went his cleats, cap, a couple of jerseys, and other baseball gear. His body shook as they disappeared into the mass of rotting garbage, but he knew it was time. No more dead weight. No more reminders. When he returned to his room, he found he had left his mitt behind on the bed and wondered why.

He grabbed it and started back outside, but a sort of force field prevented him from stepping out the door. He stared down at his glove. The same one his mom had given him so long ago. It was the best gift he ever received, but it was no longer needed. No chance of it ever sitting next to Greg Harris' in the Hall of Fame. So what was the point? Strangely, his mind refused to get involved as he folded it tight and tucked it into the bottom of his suitcase. Perhaps someday someone might have some use for it. No use throwing away good leather. Perfectly broken in. Primed and oiled. Ready to go.

Gil had always hated Phoenix, too widespread, and culturally disconnected with the rest of the state. So, when he got off at the terminal, he immediately stepped to the ticket counter and purchased a ticket heading south to Tucson—the oldest city in Arizona, and the heart and soul of the desert state. The fare was not expensive, but it left him with only his original poker stake tucked into a hidden sleeve of his wallet. He was scraping the barrel, and would have to hit the ground running.

Chapter 19

GIL FELT SELF-CONSCIOUS OVER HIS APPEARANCE. He was no longer the clean-cut ballplayer. His hair was long and unruly, chin covered with the start of a scruffy beard. He had been in Tucson two weeks with no luck in finding a job or a place to stay other than a dumpy motel. His clothes were wrinkled, demeanor downtrodden. He saw the disapproval in the eyes of the elderly, distinguished Latino man as he studied him, wondering if he was worth the risk.

"So how much do you have?"

Gil's eyes flitted left and right, avoiding contact. "Six hundred."

"That barely covers the deposit! This look like a homeless shelter?"

"No, sir. It sure don't."

"Do you have a job?"

"It won't be long."

"Like I haven't heard that before."

A young, black boy clambered up the stairs of the small apartment complex and bolted down the hallway. The old man held out a hand, palm-up, hoping to stop any interruption of his interrogation. It didn't work.

"Yo Manny! You said you would ump today. Everybody's waiting."

"My back hurts," grumbled Manny.

"Your back always hurts. I think you're faking." The kid sized up Gil. "You know anything about baseball?"

Gil quickly looked away. Manny barked, "We're busy here, Tyro! Grown-up talk."

"Ooh. I'm scared," said Tyro. "Is he the new tenant?"

"Not unless he's got more to offer." He held Gil with a stern stare.

Tyro cracked up. "You're hilarious, Manny. You don't scare anybody. Hey, you. Just tell him you need help."

"Shut up, Tyro! And I keep telling you, I am Manuel Alejandro Rodriquez Zapatero!"

"Yeah, yeah, too long," said Tyro, waving him off. He turned and slapped Gil on the arm. "Trust me. Just go on and say it."

"I think I should go," said Gil, lifting his suitcase and starting for the stairs.

Tyro looked to Manny who was trying to show how little he cared but not doing a great job of it. Tyro sighed and called out, "Yo! Are you so proud you can't ask for help when you need it? Or are you too stupid?"

"Let him go," cried Manny, halfheartedly.

Gil shoulders slumped. He stopped with his back to them. "I really do need help, mister. If you'll give me a chance, I promise I'll never miss a payment."

"Aw, geez," moaned Manny.

Tyro bounced over to Gil. "See, that wasn't so hard, was it? Old Manny is as soft an egg as they come. He can't refuse anyone who needs help. Can you Manny?"

"I oughta clobber you kid." Tyro flashed him an innocent smile of crooked, white teeth. Manny sighed. "Okay, fine. You can have the room. Give me the six hundred."

Gil pulled out the remainder of his poker stake. It felt strange giving up the bills he carried so long. His hand trembled passing them over. Tyro peered inside the wallet.

"You tapped him out, Manny! You can't leave the bro with nothin'."

"Mother Mary save me!" cried Manny. "Okay, okay, give me five hundred and you make up the difference when you get paid."

"You got a job?" asked Tyro. Gil shook his head. "He don't have no job, Manny. How's he gonna pay you? You have to help him find one."

"I do, do I? And do I also need to help him go to the bathroom?" Tyro frowned fiercely. "Easy with the death looks. I was already thinking about making some calls."

Tyro grinned and said to Gil, "Manny knows everybody. You'll get a job. Hey! I think Jaz said Billy was looking for some help."

Manny nodded. "I remember. You ever work in a restaurant?"

"That's the only kind of normal job I've ever had."

"Oh, yeah? Good deal. Okay, I'll make a call. Here's your key. You can sign the lease later. It's the one right here next to mine. And I like peace and quiet."

"Me too," said Gil.

"And don't forget, I'm not just a super, I'm the owner. Third generation. So the buck stops here. Now everybody leave me alone! I'll let you know what the restaurant says."

He slipped in his room and the door clicked shut. Tyro smiled at Gil. "Welcome home, neighbor. I live right below. Yo, I gotta go! Bros are waiting!"

He took off like a shot. Gil grinned, saying, "Thanks" to the empty hallway. He opened the apartment door. It was painfully small, with no furniture, but he exhaled a deep sigh of relief.

"I don't usually hire the white man," said Billy, member of the Pascua Yaqui Tribe, and owner of Billy's Indian Tacos. He was a giant of a man, with a stern countenance.

At Manny's instructions, Gil had come to the restaurant in hopes for a job. But now he was thinking he should make a dash for the front door. He cocked his head at the big man and asked, "Why's that?"

"I still hold a grudge." Billy's eyes narrowed, and Gil flinched. Suddenly, a wide smile appeared on the big man's face. "Just kidding. Indian humor. Actually, the reason is because most whites are lazy. I need people who work."

"You'll have no complaints, sir."

"We'll see. Anyway, you come highly recommended from Manny. And he's good people—for not being Indian, of course. My niece, Jaz, rents a room from him. You meet her yet? No? Well, just remember she's family. Hands off."

"Wouldn't think of it."

"Oh, you'll think about it. Once you see her. Unless, of course, you're in a coma, or gay. Neither one, huh? Okay. Just keep it in mind. Is grunt labor beneath you?"

"Nothing's beneath me, sir. Not anymore."

Billy studied Gil. The sincerity was undeniable, as was the strange aura of defeat surrounding him, from what source he could not tell. But it stirred something in him.

"Okay, you're hired." He crumpled up Gil's application. "And this paper means nothing. It's up to you to prove yourself."

And so he did. His duties included washing dishes and bussing tables. He attacked the work with a vengeance, to the point Billy had to tell him to slow down—he was making the slacker employees nervous.

At Billy's request, Gil shaved his face, but his hair still hung long. One of the cooks jokingly gave him a red headband, saying it would make him look more like an Indian brave, and he wore it religiously, despite the titters behind his back.

After a month of employment, and regular double shifts, he managed to pay Manny what he owed and was saving for the next month's rent. He was also proud owner of an air bed from Walmart, two chairs and a card table from Goodwill, and a small collection of cookware he discovered at a yard sale. He was almost beginning to accept the life of a normal working stiff.

Despite Tyro's incessant pleas to join the baseball games played in the vacant lot across from the complex, he steadfastly avoided his former love. When the World Series was on, Manny repeatedly invited him over to watch, but Gil deferred, preferring to sit in his room trying not to hear the muffled broadcast through the thin walls. His fingers healed as much as they ever would, however, and he began to juggle again.

One night, after a late closing at the restaurant, he struggled to find sleep. As a last resort he got out his juggling balls. It was nearly 4 a.m. and he was bounce juggling off a wall when there was a loud rapping at his door. He opened it and his breath was cut short at the sight of a statuesque, young woman scowling back at him. He was quite certain he had never seen anything so stunning.

"Do you sleep?" snapped the vision of beauty.

"When I can," mumbled Gil, trying to still his fluttering heart as he took in the long, shimmering black hair, flawless bronze skin. Her full figure alone was enough to cause a week of insomnia.

"Me, too. And right now, I can't! Whatever you're banging on the wall is driving me crazy! Now, listen closely, I work nights and sleep during the day. So far, you and I haven't had a problem. And I don't want one. So if you will kindly—"

"You're Jaz! Billy told me about you. And, man oh man, he sure wasn't kidding!"

The girl's face puckered. "About what?"

"Huh? Oh, well, he just said you were nice. I'm Gil. I work for him."

"He told me. And so did Manny and Tyro. And for future reference, my name is Jasmine. And I'm not always nice!"

Gil chuckled giddily. "I'll bet! I imagine you can be real naughty sometimes."

"Excuse me!"

"I'm sorry! Just my dumb sense of humor. I promise I'll be quiet as a mouse. I wouldn't want to interrupt your beauty sleep. That would be a real tragedy."

"Just keep it down," said Jasmine, grinning despite herself as she walked back to her room.

Gil leaned out the door. "Where do you work?"

She sighed heavily. "Casino of the Sun. The tribe owns it. And if I don't get some sleep, they'll find some other Indian to take my place. Understood?"

"Perfectly. Maybe we could do something together sometime. Lunch? Breakfast?"

"You work when I'm sleeping! Remember?"

"I'll take off! You just name the time."

She turned, ready to say no, but the sight of Gil so hopeful, and cute in a white boy kind of way, changed her mind. She smiled, and he nearly swooned. "I'll think about it. Goodnight, Gil."

"Goodnight Jasmine. By the way, I love your name!" He backed his way into his room, tripping over his feet and collapsing on his bed. "Oh, my God. I have seen an angel from heaven and I'm just waiting to die."

The next day he was still on cloud nine. For the first time since the accident, he could see a vision of the future. He didn't have much time to dwell on it, though, as the restaurant was humming. It was the annual AZ Healing Heroes Ride, a benefit for war veterans that drew bikers from around the state and beyond.

Indian tacos were always a favorite, and the stream of leather clad patrons was steady. Content in his fantasy world, Gil didn't think much of it until cleaning up a table when a large hairy paw landed on his wrist. It was Balrog.

"It's been a long time. But I'd recognize you anywhere, G-Man."

"Hey. I didn't know you were out."

"The screws got sick of me. Early parole." Gil shrugged with a half-smile, wishing he could disappear. But the biker's hardened face pinned him to the spot. "Lot of people looking for you, Gil. What are you and I going to do about that?"

"I'm not ready to go home yet. I've had a bad time."

"I heard. But is that an excuse? What about Al? And your man Tuckeroo?"

Gil shook his head, like trying to shoo away a nagging fly. "You need to keep this secret! I'll know when it's time. Will you do that for me?"

Balrog sighed. "I don't agree with it. Not at all. But I'll do it. That's what dads are for, right? Hey, don't laugh! You never know, maybe I was the one."

"Maybe. One out of six are pretty good odds."

Balrog howled and slapped the table. Billy appeared, towering over them. "You got some trouble here, Gil?"

"Nope. Just sharing a white man joke."

Billy raised an eyebrow, then moved on. Balrog said. "If there's anything you need, Gil. You just call. Here's my number. And if you know what's best for you, don't let Al hanging too long. You know how she gets."

"Yeah. Like Ice."

Balrog nodded gravely, and Gil retreated to the kitchen.

Chapter 20

A FEW DAYS BEFORE THANKSGIVING Gil showed up early at the restaurant and found the entire staff gathered for a meeting. He had not been informed, but still felt nervous as he took a place at one of the rear tables. He was hoping his arrival had gone unnoticed, but Billy immediately eyed him, a wide smile forming.

"What about you, Gil? I figure you being a new guy, we have an ace in the hole. What position do you play?"

"Sorry, boss, not sure what you're talking about."

"Baseball, what else? Our winter beer league starts soon."

Gil's lips were dry as he mumbled, "Oh, well, I'm not much for baseball, sir." He shrunk down in his seat, avoiding the shocked stares.

Billy's smile faded. "I did not ask your likes or dislikes. I asked what position you play. Think before you answer. This is mandatory. Every year we get slaughtered, but this year we're going to win it all. Because who's the meanest team in Tucson?"

On cue, the employees cried, "The Reservation Redskins!"

"See, Gil? Everybody's on board. We take this very seriously. The teams are made up of restaurants in the area. If we lose, we're the laughingstock. It affects business. Patrons want to eat at a winning establishment. And for the last three years, that Mexican joint two blocks over takes the trophy. So! Who are our sworn enemies we pledge to scalp?"

"The Barrio Banditos!" shouted the employees.

"Right on. So, Gil, please tell me you can hit."

"Not really," muttered Gil.

"Darn. So what can you do?"

"I'd rather sit it out, if it's okay with you."

A collective hush fell. Billy's face was stony as he intoned, "Okay by me. You go home now and sit it out. I'll give you a week to get back to me. You understand?"

"You firing me?"

"Call it a temporary time-out. You decide if it's permanent."

Gil couldn't believe what was happening, but he knew from Billy's scowl it was best he get out of there for the time being. He started for the door.

Billy said, "You should reconsider, Gil. Not only for your job, but if you want to make any headway with my niece, you better get on board. Jaz is crazy for baseball. She'd never think of dating a guy who didn't play."

"But I wasn't trying to get a date—"

"Don't lie. She told me all about your late-night chat. Sounds like you made a fool of yourself then. Try not to repeat it. Now get out of here."

Gil was so upset he walked aimlessly up one street and down the other, trying to calm himself. All he wanted was for baseball to drift out of his life, but now it threatened to take his job and kill any chance of being with Jasmine. By the time he wandered back to his neighborhood, hours later, he was still fuming.

The local kids were in the vacant lot starting out a game. Tyro was pitching. Gil tried skirting around, but his young neighbor spied him.

"Yo, Gil! Word's out Billy's going to can you if you don't play for the Redskins. That sucks, bro. But, I kinda see his point. Who don't play baseball? It's un-American!"

"Shut up, Tyro," barked Gil, still walking.

"No need to get harsh on a little kid! I'm just thinking I can help you out. Show you some tips. Maybe you can play first base. That's easy. Even a little girl can do that."

Gil abruptly halted, eyes flaming. He walked to Tyro and grabbed the ball. "Who's the best hitter?"

All the kids pointed to the right fielder. The boy was overly large for his age, and as he sauntered toward home plate, it was obvious he had an ego to match.

"Aw, man, you don't want to do this," said Tyro. "This guy hits everything. I should know. I never get this sucker out."

"No surprise. I've seen you pitch. All you have is a below par fastball, always middle-in where they want it, and a curve that hangs every time. Watch and learn, son."

Tyro's mouth gaped, wanting to match barb for barb, but words escaped him and Gil brushed him off the mound. The hitter got in the batter's box, sporting a wide smirk. He was a lefty, and Gil let his mind go blank, studying his stance, his mood.

"I'll give you a chance kid. First one's a slider away."

It was as if he'd never left the mound as the ball raced to the plate, the lateral break coming in the last few feet. The batter swung hard, dropping to his knees. He popped up, snarling and banging his bat in the dirt. He took his stance, more determined than ever. Gil was oblivious to the impressed chatter from Tyro and the other players.

He called, "Splitter at the knees. Gonna have to step into it." The batter tried following instructions, but swung way early.

Gil said, "Change-up coming. Wait for it."

The big kid fell for the bluff and swung too late. "That was a fastball! You said—"

"Rule Number One. Don't believe anything a pitcher tells you." Gil plopped the ball in Tyro's mitt and walked off the lot, the boys staring in disbelief.

Tyro called out, "I thought you said you didn't know nothing about baseball!"

Without looking back, Gil shouted, "I know everything there is to know, little man! I just choose not to play anymore."

"But why?! If you're that good?" Gil disappeared, and Tyro threw his arms out to his pals, looking for answers. But they had none, and slowly got back to their game.

Manny leaned back from his second-floor window. He cracked a peanut shell, fished the nut out, and popped it in his mouth. Squinting at the ceiling, he wondered who his new tenant really was.

Gil was in a quandary. For two days he wrestled with the problem. He had no desire to play ball anymore. But if he didn't, he would lose his job. He had enough to cover the next month's rent, but what about after that? There were other jobs. But what about Jasmine? Well, for that matter, there were other girls.

All he wanted was a normal life. So why was it so hard to leave the game? What did he expect coming to Tucson? It was a baseball town. They were playing in the desert when Arizona was a territory, and the U.S. Cavalry introduced the game to the area. The Cleveland Indians first held their spring training here in the 1940's, and many teams followed. It was still a regular destination for showcases and tryouts, and had been home to several Minor League teams. It now hosted the Tucson Saguaros, a proud member of the Pecos Independent league. Was it any surprise he was surrounded by baseball fanatics? So why didn't he just play and get everyone off his back?

He still had one good arm, and he was a decent lefty. There was no doubt he could compete in a little beer league, but that wasn't the point. How does one go from being brilliant to so-so and still manage to hold their head high? He always felt the game deserved the utmost respect, and that meant whoever played it must strive to live up to its exacting standards. He could no longer do that, and if he just muddled through, he'd be bringing the game down to his current level. That was unacceptable. Truth was, he couldn't stand playing the game unless he could play it to perfection.

. All his life, he had trained to pitch with both arms. And without the use of one, he was just mediocre. That was beyond the pale. He had his shot, he failed, and it was over. Nobody's fault but his own. Despite what the world was trying to do to him, he must walk away. The game would be the better for it.

With the decision made, he would now have to start over again, find a new job, forget about Jasmine, maybe even move to a new place that didn't have a lot of people trying to remind him of what was gone.

A banging on his door startled him. "It's your landlord! Open up."

"Evening, Mr. Zapatero."

"Who? Oh, yeah, that's me. But it's Manny to my tenants—and friends. Okay?" Gil nodded. "Look, I need your help. I invited some people over tomorrow for Thanksgiving, and my cooking stinks."

"So why'd you invite them over?"

"I do it every year, and every year people complain my food makes them sick. So you wonder why they come, right? Free food! Even if it's terrible, who's going to turn that down? I'm not making sense, am I? Don't worry about it. I'm old. But I'm always smelling good stuff coming from your room. So will you help me cook dinner tomorrow?"

"I'm not much for holidays. And I never cooked a traditional Thanksgiving dinner."

"Tradition be damned. Make what you want. I'll buy the food, you cook. If it stinks, I take the blame. Come on, I gave you a break, remember?"

Gil grinned. "Well, I guarantee you it won't stink. How many people?"

"Depends on who wants to brave it after last year. What a disaster. I had to hand out Pepto-Bismol. Anyway, maybe fifteen, maybe less. Is that a problem?"

"Nah. I've cooked for lots more than that. When are people showing up?"

"Around four. I thought maybe I'd go shopping now, get everything together. Do you have an idea what you want to cook?"

"I was thinking about a dish I picked up in the Dominican Republic." The words were out before Gil could stop them, and he averted his eyes, hoping to avoid questions.

"A world traveler, huh? What were you doing down there?"

"Just kicking around. Let me write out a shopping list."

The next day, Gil walked the few steps to Manny's and knocked. The door immediately swung open like he had been standing behind it, waiting.

"I gave at the office," said Manny, grinning. Gil was perplexed. "Just kidding. Come in. I'm glad you didn't chicken out. Get it? That's what we're having, right? Chicken. So I said—never mind. Nobody gets my sense of humor anyway. Let's get started."

Gil stepped in and was taken aback. The walls were covered with pennants, posters of ballplayers, and in one corner, a framed jersey with the number 15 on it. On a desk sat an old-fashioned computer, the screensaver featuring the Diamondbacks' logo. Gil immediately felt unsettled, and retreated to the small kitchen.

He went to work slicing and dicing as Manny looked on, hoping not to be asked to do anything. Which was fine with Gil. When he was cooking, he preferred to be left alone. But he could feel Manny's eyes on him and felt like he should say something.

"Are Tyro and his folks coming over?"

"Tyro's got no folks. You didn't know that? Both died in a car accident when he was three. He lives with his grandmother. Somehow, though, he's turning out alright."

"Yeah, he's a good kid."

"He thinks the world of you." Gil laughed it off. "You don't think so, huh? Then why's he always talking about you." He suddenly veered way off course, asking, "You cut with your right hand, huh? I saw you pitching with the kids the other day. You threw with your left."

Gil gritted his teeth. "Just the way I learned to throw. It's the only thing I do with my left. But I'm not real good."

"You looked damned good to me."

Gil paused mid-stroke and looked at him. "Is this about Billy, and him wanting me to play for the Redskins? Look, I can find another job. You'll get your rent for sure."

"Do I look worried? But, sure, I heard about it. And I don't see what the big deal is. It's only some beer league. They're not expecting miracles."

"Good. Because they won't be getting any from me."

"The least you could do is pitch a few games, what could it hurt?"

Gil stared hard at him. "It's personal business, Manny. I'd rather not talk about it."

"Yikes! Touchy, huh? Okay, I'll drop it. I wouldn't want to lose my chef." Gil nodded, and went back to his prep. Manny waited five seconds, then said, "So did you ever play any organized ball?"

Gil shot him an angry look, and Manny held up both hands. "Okay, okay, forget I asked. What can I do to help? Don't tell me. I know. Get out of the kitchen. Here I go. Holler if you need me. And make it loud, I'm mostly deaf!"

Manny's guests began arriving around four and Gil was ready. Dinner was not a sit-down affair as there was no table large enough, so people stood or sat with their plates in hand. He didn't know anyone except Tyro, who quickly prepared a plate and delivered it to his grandmother, as she was too old to make it up the stairs.

Most of the early birds ate and left, so by the time five rolled around, Gil was guessing the event was nearing its end. He was in the kitchen wondering what to do with the leftovers when he heard the voice of his angel—Jasmine. Oddly, he was in no mood to see her, so he continued to busy himself. The doorbell rang several times and the sounds of a whole new crowd filled the apartment.

He heard her laughing and decided he was being a fool. He stealthily moved to the doorway, hoping for a peek before he made his entrance. He heard someone ask what the main dish was.

Manny replied, "How the heck would I know? It's some sort of Latino dish." There was scattered laughter. "You'll have to ask my head chef. Hey, speak of the devil!"

Gil appeared. "It's Pollo Guisado with Wasakaka sauce."

In a corner next to Jasmine sat Billy. He paused, fork midair. "You cooked this?"

"He sure did," said Manny. "Along with everything else!"

"I didn't know you could cook," purred Jasmine. "What's wrong with you, Uncle?" She playfully head slapped him. "This man belongs in the kitchen, not washing dishes."

Billy said with mouth full, "How was I to know?!"

"I'm glad you all like it," said Gil, backstepping into the hall.

"Where you going, Gil?" asked Tyro. "Join the party!"

Gil was stuck. There was nothing to do but grab a plate and hope the evening was short. He sat cross-legged next to Tyro, and kept his head down, poking at his food. But he could feel Jasmine and Billy's eyes on him.

By six, nearly everyone was gone. Billy stretched. "Now that's a Thanksgiving dinner, Manny. And this year I won't even have to get my stomach pumped."

"Ha, ha, very funny," said Manny.

"Well, I got to get out of here, bye everyone." Jasmine elbowed him and cocked her head to Gil. Billy sighed and said, "Right. Uh, Gil, you got a second."

Gil swallowed hard and stepped over. Billy said, "I'm sorry I was a jerk. I'm just tired of the Redskins losing and hoped you could help. But just because a guy can't play ball is no reason to fire him. And Jasmine is right, I'd like you in the kitchen from now on. I'll start you prepping and move you to the grill when a spot opens up. It means a raise."

Gil couldn't believe it. He stuck out his hand and Billy shook it firmly. "Thanks, boss." He turned to Jasmine, and said, "And I sure wish I could be the kind of guy you wanted. More than anything. But I understand how you feel."

"What are you talking about?"

"You not being interested in any guy who's not a ballplayer."

Billy tried to slip by in a quick move for the door, but Jasmine grabbed him by the shirt. "Did you tell him that?!"

"Well, I, um, maybe, but—"

She slugged him hard in the pecs and he winced. "I just thought it might sway him a little. I mean I knew he was hot for you and—"

"Get out of here, you big dope! And don't ever do that again!"

He ducked his head, slinking to the door. "See you Monday, Gil?"

"Sure, boss," said Gil with a grin. After he was gone, there was an awkward moment. Gil broke it with, "So you really don't like baseball, Jasmine?"

"Of course I like it. You can't live in my family and not. Some distant relative, Moses Yellow Horse played two years for the Pirates. Since then, every boy in the extended family has tried following his footsteps. But it's not like I check out a guy's batting average before I date him."

"So, maybe someday—"

"Not maybe. Definitely." She smiled coyly. "One thing I can always use is a man who can cook. I stink at it, just like Manny."

"Hey!" cried Manny. "Only I'm allowed to say that!"

Jasmine laughed and said, "I've got to get to work. Bang on my wall sometime, Gil. But not too early!" She gave him a peck on the cheek, and hurried out the door.

Gil was downright giddy. Life was looking up again! He turned back to the room and saw Manny and Tyro frowning at him.

"You're off the hook, huh?" asked Manny. "You got your job back, and a chance at Jasmine. And you don't even have to play ball. Lucky you."

"I told you, I don't play."

"Sure you do," said Tyro. "You said you knew everything there was to know."

"Just talk. I used to follow the game as a kid, like you. But that was years ago. I couldn't help Billy's team if I tried."

There was a long silence, during which Manny seemed to make some sort of decision. He heaved himself out of his easy chair and said, "You guys are going to help to clean up, right? I thought so. While we're at it, let's play a little baseball trivia."

"Right on!" cried Tyro grabbing up plates. "I got one. Who was the only Major Leaguer with one arm, what was his position, and who did he play for?"

"Unfair!" announced Manny. "That's three questions. But it doesn't matter, because I know it anyway. It was Pete Gray, centerfielder for the St. Louis Browns. And for an added bonus, his only big league season was in 1945."

Gil was secretly impressed. He knew of Gray, but not the year he played.

"You're up, Gil," said Tyro.

"I forget most of what I knew. You fellas go on."

"No way! Think harder!"

"Alright, who was the oldest pitcher to throw a perfect game, and how old was he?"

"Way too easy!" exclaimed Tyro. "Randy Johnson, age forty, against the Braves on May 18, 2004. You gotta do better than that! This is serious business."

Gil was surrounded by trivia sharks, and had to dig deep into his vast resources. "Here you go. Who was the youngest MLB player of all time, and how old was he?"

They gathered around the sink and Manny and Tyro were momentarily stumped.

"Give up?" asked Gil, a little too smugly.

"Hold on, I know this one," said Manny. "Joe somebody. Joe Nuxhill!"

"Nuxhall," corrected Gil. "But close enough. How old?"

"Sixteen?" asked Manny.

"Huh-uh. Fifteen."

Tyro shouted, "That's a good one. You even beat Manny. That's almost impossible."

"Relax, kid," said Manny. "Here's a real poser. About seven, eight years ago, who pitched a three-hit shutout for the Toowoomba Rangers to clinch the Australian Pacific League Championship. And here's a hint. He did it with both arms."

"A switch-pitcher? Whoa!" cried Tyro. "But it's not fair, that's international ball."

"I think it is," said Manny, looking at Gil staring into the sink of sudsy water. "What do you think, Gil. Is that a fair question?" Gil shrugged. "So tell us. Who is it?"

"That would be me, of course."

Chapter 21

"G-MAN?!" SHOUTED TYRO. "That's who you are?"

He was seated in front of Manny's computer looking at Gil's website. Manny was over his shoulder. Gil was slumped on the couch.

"That's me," he mumbled. "Or was. How long you known about this, Manny?"

"A couple days. After I saw you pitching with the kids, I got curious and looked your name up."

"Yo! You've played all over the world!" exclaimed Tyro, spinning to Gil. "Why would you keep this a secret? If I could pitch like you, I'd be telling everybody!"

"Simple. I don't pitch like that anymore."

Manny took a place next to him. "Yeah, I read about the injury. So the right arm's no good anymore, huh? Pitches aren't flying good?"

Gil shrugged. "I haven't even bothered trying to use it. What's the point?"

"Geez, I don't know. To see if it works?"

Gil shook his head. "People always talk about how healthy a pitcher's arm is. But it's not the arm that's important. It's the fingers. And just look at 'em!"

"They still grip, right? I saw you cutting with them."

"Yeah, but that's not enough. It's how the ball comes off them that's important."

"So, the old pitches won't work. What about new ones?"

Gil smirked. "You don't understand."

"Hm. Maybe not."

Tyro said, "Why not just use your left arm? Southpaws are always in demand."

Gil sighed heavily. "A long time ago I chose to be a switch-pitcher, one like the game had never seen. I spent all my time learning which arm was best in any given situation. Without both, I'm just run-of-the-mill."

There was silence until Manny said, "In this one post by your buddy Tucker, he tells how you became a switch-pitcher. It took a lot of guts and strength to reinvent yourself. And at such a young age."

"It wasn't easy."

"Uh-huh. So why is it so hard now?"

Tyro said, "Yeah! Why can't you do that now?"

Gil frowned and shot off the couch. "You just won't listen. Neither of you! My time is over! And there's nothing I can do about it. Even if I were to learn to use these damn fingers, it wouldn't make a difference."

Manny said, "You'd be a switch-pitcher again. That's what you want, right?" Gil began to pace. "I bet I know your problem. You're one of those perfectionists. If everything isn't exactly the way you want it, then it's not good enough at all."

"That ain't it! Hell, I was always a junk dealer. Nothing I threw was perfect. I just tossed what I knew would work. And usually it did."

"Then stop messing around!" said Tyro. "You need to get back to the game."

"For what? Even if I do get both arms going again, who's gonna want me?"

"What about all those teams you played for?" cried Tyro. "Eight years it said you played year-round ball. That's a lot of people who wanted you then."

Gil spit out a puff of air. Manny said, "I know what it is. Like a lot of players, the only success for you is getting in the majors. Everything else is worthless."

"Well isn't it?!" cried Gil, leaning into him, face inches away.

"I don't think so. Tyro and his pals take their games as seriously as any pro. So do the Redskins. Baseball is the same game no matter where it's played, or who plays it."

Gil spun away from him and angrily kicked the base of the closest chair.

Manny continued. "It's not that I don't understand your feelings. When you're as good as you, you want to play with the best. You want to be on top. It's only natural."

"That's right!" said Gil. "But they just don't want me. Believe me I've tried!"

"I know. I read everything on your site. The complete history. Seems to me, though, you might have quit a little early."

"I didn't quit! I was hurt!"

"Sure, but right before that, you played with the most respected Independent League in the country. That's no mean feat."

Tyro said. "And that one game in the Caribbean Series, you got thirteen guys out in a row. You know how many players go to the big leagues straight out of that series?"

"Yeah, I do! And despite me pitching like a god, nobody had any interest!"

Manny said, "So, even if you hadn't gotten injured, you were ready to quit anyway."

Gil froze, mouth open, ready to attack, but the truth held him back. He walked to Manny's easy chair and plopped down. "Maybe," he muttered. "Started thinking about how I was wasting my life, with no chance of success."

Manny closed his eyes and leaned back, folding his hands on his lap. "Quitting. It's an age-old story. As old as dreaming. Thank God my wife never had that problem. In fact, if she were here, she'd put you over her lap and give you a good spanking."

"Your wife! What would she know about all this?" asked Gil, disgustedly.

Tyro popped to his feet. "Shut up man! You're talking about Rose." He shot a finger out to the framed jersey. "Number fifteen."

"She played ball?"

Manny nodded, like he was falling asleep. "Right field and pitcher. One of the first players to join the All-American Girls Professional Baseball League during World War II. Started with the Rockford Peaches and helped them win the League Championship in '45, '48 and '49. Then she got traded to the Kalamazoo Lassies. Then the men came home, and the league disbanded in '54."

Gil muttered, "So she was real good, huh?"

Manny grinned sadly. "Never got to see her play, except in practice. But she was considered one of the best all-around woman players of her time. She was fifteen years older than me. When the league ended, she moved here to be close to tryouts and spring camps. I saw her practicing one day, right out in that field out there. And that was it. I was in love. I guess she was too. It was a big scandal back then—with my family anyway. Marrying a white girl, and so much older than me. But what a gal."

"So she never got to play again?"

"Nowhere to play. And she refused to sink to amateur. She just kept petitioning the majors to allow women in. But they never did, and never have. She knew all about fighting tradition and she never stopped. No matter what. One year, she even cut her hair, dressed up like a guy and went to tryouts for the Indians. They caught her. Just about broke her heart. But even after that she wouldn't give up."

"Didn't you try stopping her?"

"No way. Some people are born with a dream. I never had one. My grandfather owned this dump, then my father, then me. It was all I ever needed, or wanted. When I met her, I realized there was a different breed out there. And the way I figured, the job for people like me was to support the dreamers. That's what they need. Blind loyalty."

Gil shook his head. "I still think you should've saved her from it."

Manny's eyes popped open. "You're not listening! You take away the dream and it's slow suffocation! It would've killed her."

Gil mulled this over. "When did she die?"

"Young," said Manny, getting to his feet. "I'd like for you to go now, Gil. I'm sorry I uncovered your secret and I won't bother you anymore. You've made your decision. Now you get to live with it. But not around us. Next thing you know, you'd be turning Tyro into a quitter."

"That's not fair!" yelled Gil, leaping to his feet.

"You're right. Somebody else should've been given your talent. Now get out."

Gil's face turned beet red. He sputtered and tried arguing, but Manny took him by the elbow and led him to the door. With a light shove, he was in the hallway and stomped back to his room.

For some time, he silently raged. Alone and unsure, his mind filled with a flurry of scattered, disconnected thoughts. He grabbed his juggling balls and using his right arm began hurling them into the adjoining wall to Manny's apartment. One after the other. Over and over. For hours.

Manny patiently listened to the incessant thumping. Tyro quickly tired of it, and retired to his apartment. Manny settled into his easy chair and waited.

Midnight was closing in when the sound finally stopped. Manny opened his eyes, wondering what was next. He heard footsteps, then a knock. "It's open."

Gil stepped in. "I need to borrow your phone."

"Get your own."

Gil steadied his breathing. "I have to talk to my catcher. Please, sir."

Manny studied him, then tossed over his cell. Gil dialed and waited.

"Tuck. It's me." He wandered into the hallway and Manny could only hear parts of the muffled conversation. After several minutes, Gil reappeared.

"Okay, buddy. I'll see you tomorrow." He hung up and handed the phone to Manny. "Thanks."

He headed for the door, and Manny said, "What changed your mind?"

Gil turned, a grim smile appearing. "Number Fifteen."

Bottom of the 7th

I HAD JUST ABOUT GIVEN UP ON THIS LITTLE BOOK, and the journey for that matter. I convinced myself a simple injury was enough reason to walk away from everything I was fighting for. Fortunately, two new friends, one young and one old, decided to set my mind straight. They did it by introducing me to a fine lady. She's dead now, but in her day she fought a battle that made mine look like a pillow fight. She never won. But she made me see it wasn't winning that makes a good warrior, it's the unwillingness to accept defeat. I'll never forget her. In fact, I've come to think of her as my lucky charm. If a woman can spit in the eye of a giant and not flinch or run away, then so can I.

I look back and wonder how I could've been so silly. I actually believed there was a path I could take to live happily ever after like other people. But I'm different, and there is no hiding from it. So, I'm back, and I swear I'm not giving an inch until my arms truly are no longer capable of pitching. That's the way it is, and the way it's going to be.

Tucker, as always, has been a big help. He was the first person to come running once I returned to my normal self.

At first, he seemed to think my problem was his fault, but I set him straight. He was relieved, not leastwise that I was back chasing the dream.

It was a funny moment when I first showed him my deformed fingers. I played it up real big, whining how none of my pitches would ever work again, and on and on. He just sat there, real calm the way he is. And when I was done with my tantrum, he looked closely at my right hand, and said, "Looks like a perfect knuckleball grip to me."

I laughed so hard, about fell off my chair. But he just kept staring at me, straight-faced, which made me laugh even more. But, as usual, he was right. We started off practicing, and using a two-knuckle grip, I got it down pat. Of course, I hardly ever know where the ball is going, but then again, neither do the batters. Or the umpire or catcher for that matter! But I've calculated as long as I get it in the strike zone at least 30% of the time, those batters just can't lay off. That's the beauty of the knuckleball. I believe even "Candy Man" Candiotti, "Old Sarge" Wilhelm, and "Dutch" Leonard would be impressed. It's become my primary pitch for my right arm, although I found the bent fingers actually help with a couple others. I got a forkball to set up my knuckler, and am working on a screwball, which breaks away from the lefties, like a left-handed curveball. Nasty stuff.

Tuck started coming down every weekend, and after Christmas spent two weeks. Since then, he's been coming regular, even during the week. I worried about him taking off so much work, but he said this was more important. Work could wait.

To try out my new stuff, I've been playing in a local league. My coach, who's actually my boss where I work, has been real helpful. When I was in my funk, I told him I couldn't play ball at all. After I recovered from my stupidity, I told him the truth and he was like a kid on Christmas morning. I imagine that's in part because our team is winning big, especially when I pitch, which is nearly every game.

I asked him to help get my legs back in shape, and he's had no problem with me bunting for base and trying to steal second when I can. And he's just thrilled with my being a switch-pitcher. He gets a real hoot out of it, and has been doing his best to tell the world what a gem he has. He's got a big spread of me up on his restaurant's website, and says they've never had such crowds at their games. I've been tickled helping his team win. I guess I've always been a fan of underdogs. I just can't seem to get enough of them.

Everywhere I turn, I'm finding people who want to help me succeed. One, in particular, needs mentioning. Her name is Jasmine. We first met when I was still in a fog, and I saw her as the answer to my problem. She was to be my wife, and I would find comfort hiding behind her skirt. Of course, at the time, she knew nothing about this, as it was a private fantasy. In fact, I could barely get her to look at me. Later, after I started pitching again, she stopped by my place one night, and I could tell she was in the mood for loving. Well, I made my move, but midway, my conscience started biting. I had already told her I was no ballplayer, and she was alright with that. Well, I fessed up and suddenly the cozy moment was over.

She told me anything that might happen between us would have to wait. I thought she was angry at me for lying, but it wasn't so. She explained that her people (she's Indian) were used to fighting the tough fights. And the worst thing for a warrior was to be distracted. She said she would not be responsible for taking my mind off the goal. Well, at first I was real disappointed. But it came to make sense. Because there is no doubt my lovely Jasmine is a walking, talking distraction of the first degree.

Lucky for me, she made it clear in no way was she shutting me out forever. She swore we would remain the closest of friends and would support me through thick and thin. She has made good that promise. She's rearranged her work schedule to be at all the games. At times, I can see a gleam in her eyes when she watches me pitch, and I know someday our time will come. And I keep her in mind when I go out on the mound. I'm determined to be her Indian brave for as long as she's still got eyes for me. She might settle for someone who doesn't always win, but never for one who doesn't fight the good fight, as Danny likes to say.

Speaking of him, Tuck said he'd been looking high and low for me. Seems he's given up the law and has become a sports agent. At first, I didn't want to talk to him until I had gotten back up to speed, but Tuck convinced me otherwise.

We had a good chat the other day, and he has some notion the new rule changes will help my chances of getting picked up by a big league team. At first, I was skeptical, but when he starts talking like a preacher it's tough to argue. He wants to represent me, but says I need to prove myself to his boss, who's some bigwig in the agent business.

He says if I can get myself into an Independent League this summer, he'll be able to prove I should be represented by their firm. Once that happens, he says he'll talk me up to teams and try to stir up some action. He is convinced once it's realized how difficult it is to adapt to the new pitching rule, teams will be scrambling to come up with a solution, that's when I'll be looking like gold. His goal is to have me on a team before the end of the season.

It all sounds a little too rosy to me, but I sure am happy to have him on my side. I told him I'll do whatever it takes and whatever he tells me. Privately, I'm still hoping to get picked up during tryouts this spring and avoid all these complications. But if not, I'll make damn sure to get into an Independent League. I have a lot of connections from past teams, and they may help me out.

Anyway, that's where things stand. I've got a game to get to. It's the championship against our sworn enemies, those darned Barrio Banditos. I'm not too worried, though. I'm the starter, and once I get through with them, they'll most likely choose to take up badminton or maybe pickle ball next year. Something where there's no fear of their fragile egos getting hurt. Ha Ha!

Chapter 22

GIL WAS IN FOR A SURPRISE. He had no idea Tucker was bringing the whole family to the game. Danny was also there. Gil didn't know any of this until afterwards when the crowd spilled onto the field to celebrate his no-no. It wasn't the first no-hitter he'd pitched, but it was perhaps the sweetest. Throughout, he had switched arms effortlessly, and if not for one walk it would have been a perfect game.

Billy's glee was uncontrollable as he howled at the top of his lungs making the Banditos feel worse than they already did. Jasmine smothered Gil with kisses. Manny and Tyro danced around the mound with Gil's family. Skip was thrilled to finally see his uncle pitch. Danny just sat in the stands, seeing visions of future glory.

There was another witness to the event who was taken completely by surprise at Gil's performance. That roving bird dog scout, JJ Jaggard, had heard whispers of a local hero in Tucson claiming to be a switch-pitcher. He had no idea it was the same player he had seen less than a year earlier. He was stunned Gil had recovered so quickly. He was even more startled to see how he had adapted to the injured fingers. But when he watched him pitch the full nine innings with no batter coming close, he was in awe. It was only amateur ball, but he had been too long in the business not to trust in his gut. This was no fluke. Gil was a true phenom.

Moments after the last pitch, he was on his phone. "Ollie. JJ. I'm in Tucson. Your boy has resurfaced. Believe it or not, he's back on the mound. I gotta hand it to you, you knew all along the kid had it, and you were right. He pitched a no-no today using both arms. It was just some local league, but I'd stake money he could do it at any level, including the bigs. What's that? Yeah, it's a problem. I can't contact any of my people until I can show him off, and not in some beer league. Anything you can do on your end for this summer? Alright, let me know. It doesn't have to be much, just so it's pro ball. And one other thing. This guy's fun to watch. Real fun. We both know what that means. Guaranteed crowds. Keep it in mind if you're thinking the D-backs. Talk soon."

He hung up and noticed there was a young, dapper man sitting right behind him. "Good game, huh? Kid can pitch."

"I know," said Danny. "Who are you? And who were you just talking to?"

"It was a private conversation."

"That's the problem with cell phones, no privacy anymore. So back to my questions." Danny slid down next to him.

"First of all, who are you?"

"I know Gil."

"So you're a friend, so what?"

"More than that. I represent him."

JJ wrinkled his brow. "You some kind of freelance shark?"

"Not exactly. I work with Abe Scally. Ring a bell?"

JJ leaned back. Scally changed everything. "You mean he's actually signed with Scally?"

"It's in the works. Now tell me who you were talking to."

JJ was not surprised at the turn of events. No one with real talent can hide forever. "His name is Ollie Denning."

"His old coach. Gil told me about him. First guy that believed in him."

"Yeah. Well, after today, you've got another believer. Name's JJ Jaggard."

Danny smiled. Jaggard's name was legendary for the overlooked players he had discovered. He held out a hand. "Danny Kane. Can we talk?"

JJ said with a grin, "I think we should."

Spring bloomed early that year, and by the time it arrived Gil was in top form. He was, therefore, quite peeved when politely asked by his supporters not to attend tryouts. Danny, JJ, and Denning had combined forces to become his triumvirate. For weeks, they had plotted a strategy for his latest assault on the MLB, and it did not include open tryouts, which they believed were a waste of his time.

They determined the best place to show off his talent was in an Independent League where he could completely dominate. Statistics also showed pitchers in the Independent Leagues had a 40% better chance over position players of getting signed midseason by MLB teams. Due to injuries, pitchers were always in demand.

Privately, Danny had other reasons why he wanted Gil in the Independents. By keeping him free of any ties to an affiliated team, he would be strategically positioned when the time was ripe to strike—when the need for his talents was at its peak. He was playing a high-stakes game of poker, and everything depended on being right about the upcoming rule change. If he was wrong, Gil might well sit out another season. But Danny didn't just want him picked up by some team and sent to the minors for years on end. In one fell swoop, he was hoping to shoot him to the top of the heap.

He, JJ, and Ollie were still in the process of deciding which league and team to focus on when the answer was thrust upon them. The owner of the Tucson Saguaros heard about Gil's success with the Redskins and was actively seeking him out.

The Saguaros had only been formed a few years earlier as an expansion franchise with the Pecos League, a relative newcomer to the Independent Leagues. The owner's head scout tracked Gil down at Billy's Indian Tacos and was referred to Danny.

Both JJ and Denning approved of the choice as it would keep Gil readily accessible to the Diamondbacks' base of operations in Phoenix. Gil would have happily agreed to be on any MLB team, but his lifelong love of the D-backs made them his first choice. Having Denning on the inside—with the possibility of swaying decisions, helped seal the deal. With their target fixed firmly in their sights, they let Danny loose to negotiate with the Saguaros.

Owners of baseball teams in the outlaw leagues, are notoriously fickle—for good reason. The margin of error between turning a profit and realizing a loss is razor thin. It seemed at the onset Gil was a shoo-in. The owner knew of his fan appeal, guaranteeing ticket sales, but he still demanded he demonstrate his pitching against known hitters.

It was a temporary setback, but Danny rallied, contacting the two power hitters he had signed for his agency. Both were in spring training, one with the Padres the other the Mariners, but they agreed to help. Fortunately, both teams held their training in Peoria, a suburb of Phoenix, where the spring Cactus League held games. Word got around and a few other players who knew Gil volunteered to assist.

To make things easier on the hitters, Danny and Gil traveled with the owner and his manager to a community ballpark outside Phoenix. It was a hot Sunday, and the first person Gil saw was Tucker. Danny had arranged for him to function as catcher, knowing it would calm his 'racehorse' and give him an edge.

Aside from an umpire hired for the session, five batters were scheduled to show. Danny's two clients were unfamiliar to Gil, but he recognized two of the others. They were Venezuelan players who had recently been drafted. He had faced them in the Caribbean Series, and snuffed both out. It dawned on him they volunteered only to get back at him. He wasn't bothered in the least. The last hitter showed up a little late, and as he hopped out of his car, Gil let out a whoop.

"Chip Benson!" cried Gil. "Well, I'll be damned! How the heck are you?"

Chip jogged up and gave him a bear hug. "Never better buddy!"

"Where you playing?"

"Still with the Padres. Triple A. But if I keep going the way I am, I think they're finally going to move me out of the parking lot and up to the majors this year."

"Nobody deserves it more than you!"

"Except you! Hell, I wouldn't have even been drafted if it weren't for you."

"Still closing your eyes?"

Chip laughed. "Naw. But you taught me to feel the hit, Gil. Trust in it, quiet the brain, all that stuff! I never forgot it, and if there's anything I can ever do for you, just ask."

"Well, you're doing it right now. But you got to promise not to strike out on purpose."

Chip slapped him on the back. "Friends are friends, but that would be asking too much." He leaned into Gil, and said conspiratorially, "I can't believe nobody's picked you up yet. When I heard you had a private tryout, I figured it was for a real team. Why you messing around with this little Pecos League?"

Gil grinned. "It's been a long ride, man. And it's not going to stop here. I have an agent now, and he's got a long-term plan. I hope to be up there with you soon."

"That'd be great! As long as it's not one of the other teams in the NL West! We'd be in trouble then!"

The owner of the Saguaros was getting impatient, so Danny politely broke up the reunion and got things rolling. The hitters would bat in rotation, each facing Gil two times. As the first batter came up, Danny started filming with his phone. He foresaw this tryout as valuable down the road. Gil was facing rising players who were drawing attention around the league. If he could face them down, people would take notice.

Tucker and Gil had been practicing so much they were in perfect sync. Also, Tucker had painstakingly researched each player, and knew precisely what to call. Despite the increasing heat of the day, Gil barely broke a sweat before the thing was over. The total damage amounted to three softly hit grounders that never made it out of the infield, two lazy pop-ups, and a whistling line drive hit by Chip— the only bona fide hit of the day. In-between were a ton of foul balls, and four strikeouts. Gil had switched arms six times.

When it was over, the Saguaros' manager was practically salivating, urging his boss to sign Gil. Danny thanked the hitters for coming and they all drifted off except for Chip, who huddled with Tucker and Gil.

"Sorry about that last one," said Chip. "It was a lucky swing."

"Don't you be apologizing!" said Gil, laughing. "I'll get you next time."

"No doubt! I only hope it's in the show. See you around, G-Man!"

The owner of the Saguaros waved Danny over and sized him up. "You got something you want to tell me?"

"Like what?" asked Danny innocently, a twinkle in his eye.

"Doesn't make sense. Those guys he just embarrassed are no slouches. Your boy's an ace. Why's he still in Independent ball?"

"That's the million-dollar question. You want him or not?"

"Oh, I want him! Mom didn't raise an idiot. But you've got something cooking. You're grooming him. And the Saguaros are the showcase. Am I right?" Danny shrugged, noncommittedly. "Uh-huh. Well, I'll tell you what. I'll play along. But I want a healthy payoff clause if he gets picked up during the season."

"I'll go twice his contract. No higher. With a written guarantee he's a starter. No burying him in the bullpen. I need to have him seen. And he's a switch-pitcher. You mess with that, he walks."

The owner chuckled. "You been at this long?"

"Long enough to know when I've struck gold."

"I'll bet. Okay, you got yourself a deal. And just between you and me, you have yourself one helluva pitcher."

"Let's hope it doesn't stay a secret."

Chapter 23

THE SAGUAROS HELD THEIR SPRING TRAINING on the Pascua Pueblo Yaqui Reservation, near the Casino of the Sun. Jasmine changed to day shift so she could be on a similar schedule as Gil. During breaks, she and fellow employees came to watch the workouts. He was already known by the tribe through his friendship with her, working at Billy's and his success with the Redskins. But as the start of the season neared, many members unofficially adopted him as one of their own.

On opening day, he started against the Bakersfield Train Robbers. The Saguaros played their home games at Cherry Field and the stands were filled to capacity. Most had come solely to see Gil, and they were not disappointed.

The game was a rout in favor of the Saguaros, and it was to be an indicator of Gil's ascendancy that summer. Like his supporters suspected, the competition was outmatched. The owner was ecstatic, and knowing Gil's tenure might be short-lived, he played it to the hilt. By the second game, *G-Man*, was plastered on T-shirts, caps and pennants. Interviews for local radio and television shows followed. Gil's pre-game warm-up was highly touted, and fans showed up early just to see him juggle.

By June, he was a local celebrity and people flocked to Billy's Indian Tacos to meet him. Despite his community fame, he still needed to work a regular job, as the pay for the Saguaros was capped at $50 a week. Billy made sure, however, his star employee did not go without. His pay was doubled, and for the most part his job was to mingle with the customers and be seen.

Behind the scenes, Danny worked closely with Tucker. He knew his hand would be stronger when he made his move if Gil had a formidable online presence. Out of his own pocket, he created a budget for Google AdWords, and Tucker launched a campaign targeting specific keywords. He rallied Gil's fan base, urging them to click through to the website and Facebook page. Regular blog posts relayed his recent triumphs, with video footage of highlights. By July, anyone searching his name, G-Man, or switch-pitcher, found his website at the head of the list, topping Venditte and Greg Harris. Word was spreading.

On other fronts, the news was promising. As predicted, many MLB teams were nonplussed over the new pitching rule change. Teams were digging deep into their farm systems to find a solution. Most were failing. The D-backs were no exception. They started out the season with a shaky roster at best, and due to attrition, were already calling pitchers up from the minors. As the trade deadline loomed, there was talk of trading their top ace, whose immense salary was preventing them from acquiring necessary relievers.

Top management was loathe to proceed, however, because despite their pitching woes, they were in possession of several top hitters and the team was stubbornly hanging tight in the wildcard race.

Unfortunately, the division had once again been wrapped up early by the deep pocket Dodgers.

A week before the trade deadline, the D-backs lost five in a row, and despite their misgivings they traded their headliner. It was a blow to the players. They assumed the front office decided to write off the season and begin a rebuilding process. The GM, however, was not a man to give up on a team with such potential. He was cagey, knowing with the right strategic moves, and the freed-up monies from the trade, his team might just be capable of making a run for it.

He sent word through the network of scouts he was looking for arm talent and didn't care where it came from. With the trade deadline past, it left non-tendered, unrestricted free agents. This included former players who were either sitting on the couch having been passed over that year, or didn't get picked up on waivers, as well as overlooked players buried in the International and Independent Leagues.

JJ quickly heard the news from his contacts and Denning confirmed it. When Danny found out, he knew all he had planned for was coming to a head. He convinced Abe Scally to officially sign Gil to the agency and the game was afoot.

The Saguaros' regular season ended the day before the trade deadline, and they sailed into the playoffs with the best record in the league. Gil trusted wholly in Danny but he was antsy. The whole idea was to get one of the Diamondbacks' scouts to see him in action, and the chance for that was drawing to a close. Danny said not to worry. The trigger was cocked, waiting for the right moment to be pulled.

After the Saguaros won the first round playoffs, Danny decided it was time to act. Initially, he hoped the

D-backs would discover Gil on their own, but it was time to give them a nudge in the right direction. He called JJ and told him what he needed. JJ did not hesitate to call one of his contacts who put him in touch with a top D-back scout.

"Stan Atchison. JJ Jaggard here."

"Hey, JJ. Bill said you have someone I should look at. Music to my ears. The front office is breathing down my neck, and Bill swears by you. So is he a righty or lefty?"

"Both."

"Excuse me."

"He's a switch-pitcher."

"Aw, geez. They'll never go for it."

"Just see for yourself, Stan. If you're sold on him, they'll at least have to listen. He's in Tucson with the Saguaros. But don't let that fool you, he's for real, and he's proven it all over the world. For whatever reasons, the majors have overlooked him. Do yourself a favor. He's pitching tomorrow in the playoffs. Cherry Field. Seven o'clock. I'll hold a ticket at the gate for you. I'll be behind home plate."

There was a long pause, then, "I'll see if I can make it, JJ. Thanks for the call."

It was the bottom of the first and JJ figured his sales pitch had failed. The only empty seat in the stands was the one next to him, with no sign of Stan. Gil jogged out to the mound and the crowd erupted. He tipped his cap and the women swooned. Every pitch he threw was met with roars of approval. After quickly mowing down the first three batters, the audience began chanting his moniker. Stan suddenly appeared, shouldering his way through the raucous fans. He plopped next to JJ and gave him a quizzical look.

"This is nuts!"

"I should've warned you," said JJ with a grin. "Too bad you missed his first inning."

"Oh, I saw it!" said Stan. "I just couldn't fight my way down here. The kid is like some rock star."

"Yeah, he packs them in. For good reason. So why'd you decide to show?"

"You. I did my research. You have quite the track record. What's your secret?"

JJ smiled broadly. "Call it a knack."

Midway through the game, Gil came to the plate and bunted. It was an obvious sacrifice, meant to move the man from first into scoring position. Gil had other notions and beat out the throw.

"Are you kidding me?!" cried Stan.

"Oh, I forgot to mention. He's real fast."

"He's faster than fast for God's sake! No pitcher does that."

"It gets better."

Right then, Gil and the man on second made their move, pulling off a clean double steal. Stan, jaw flapping, turned to JJ who shrugged. "Like I said."

Stan blinked hard, and immediately started jotting down notes in his notebook. At the end of the eighth, Gil jogged off the mound. His pitch count was 82. So far, no one had managed to cross the plate.

"Is he always this good?" asked Stan.

"I haven't seen a well-hit ball all season. Dribblers, infield pop-ups, lazy fly balls. I hate to say I told you so."

"Brag all you want! You've made a believer out of me."

The game was soon over with the Saguaros advancing to the Championship Series. Stan hurried off, promising to do his best. Danny had been seated several rows back watching Stan and JJ. Now he slipped through the stands and sat in Stan's vacated seat. "Was he impressed?"

"Who wouldn't be? Your boy's a cool customer. Lot of guys freeze up when they know the pressure is on."

Danny smiled. "When I told him he might be here, he asked if he should wear a tie."

JJ grinned and shook his head. "Figures."

"So what do you think?"

JJ shrugged. "Oh, we'll get our plug. But how much clout Stan's got, who knows? Now it's a waiting game. Though it might be time to forewarn Ollie. Bring a little pressure to bear. Without being obvious, of course."

"Naturally," said Danny with a grin.

Denning was receptive to Danny's request, and at a meeting with the manager of the Reno Aces, brought up Gil's name as a possible late recruit. The Diamondbacks had attempted to bolster their bullpen, and it still hadn't worked. It was clear if they didn't do something quickly, the chances of making a serious September run were over. The front office was open to suggestions. When Denning brought Gil up to his manager at the meeting, however, the notion of a switch-pitcher was labelled outlandish and rejected outright.

The same day, on August 11, Gil led the Saguaros to a championship. The season was officially over, and still no word from the Diamondbacks.

Two weeks later, after a day game with the Aces, Denning sat in his living room and watched the last hour of the D-backs against the Giants. Going into the bottom of the ninth Arizona was up by two runs. The current closer, a lefty, had been shaky at best, and this game was no exception. He walked the first two men. The third was a rookie but known as a left-handed power hitter. Normally, the manager would have replaced the pitcher for a righty, but the new rule disallowed it.

The rookie wasted no time. The first pitch was launched over the right field wall— his first MLB walk-off home run. San Francisco was currently last in the division, and it was a game Arizona could ill afford to lose.

Ollie Denning's eyes narrowed. He was already testy. The Aces had lost another game that day and were close to being eliminated. On top of it, he had been ignored by his manager at the recent meeting. The game he just watched made him even more ill-tempered. He leaned back in his chair and closed his eyes.

Baseball is an unpredictable game, and anyone who says what will or will not work in any given situation is treading on thin ice. Coaches and managers lose their jobs all the time for acting on their instincts and trying to manipulate outcomes. On the other hand, that's what they're paid to do, and the risks come with the job. Anyone in such a position has to stand behind what they believe— or find a new occupation.

Ollie's eyes snapped open. He grabbed his phone and dialed. "Danny. Any news?"

"No. I'm not sure what to do next. September is a few days away. Any ideas?"

"Maybe. The guys you rounded up to hit against Gil for that tryout. There were a couple of Venezuelans in the mix."

"Sure. Gil said he pitched against them in the Caribbean Series. They didn't do much better against him in Phoenix."

"Right. You remember their names?"

"Hold on, I've got the list on my desk. Here we go. There was a Montilla."

"No, he's with the Athletics now. Who was the other one?"

"Gallegos."

"That's him. I knew it sounded familiar. Just wanted to confirm. He just made a fool out of the Diamondbacks' latest closer to win a game that should've been a lock. It's time someone sees what Gil would've done to him. So I need you to send me the video file of those tryouts."

"I see where you're going, and I'll do better! I'll email you the whole thing now, but give me twenty minutes and I'll edit out Gallegos' at-bats and send those as a separate clip. But can you get them to somebody who can a make a difference?"

"How does the top dog sound?"

"You're kidding."

"I'm tired of messing around. What's the use of me being in the organization if I can't go straight to the boss. I'll email him the Gallego video as soon as I get it, then I'm taking a late flight to Phoenix so I'll have tomorrow open. Aces have a day off."

"You sure you can get a meeting that quick?"

Denning grinned. "After he sees the tape, he'll be the one demanding a meeting. If JJ's in the area ask him to be on stand-by. And tell him to give Stan a heads-up. I'm sure he'd like to be in on it. His pitch for Gil was obviously ignored, just like mine. No scout likes that. Neither do I."

"You got it Ollie! Look, I'm in L.A. but I'm booking a red-eye as we speak. If lightning strikes our boy's going to need representation. You realize you're sticking your neck out there? I'd hate to see it get chopped off over this."

"All for a good cause. G-Man deserves better. And I'm a sucker for an underdog."

Chapter 24

"THE VIDEO WAS IMPRESSIVE, OLLIE. But it was just one guy. Why should I care?" The Diamondbacks' GM leaned back in his chair behind his large, stainless steel desk.

"Because there's more, if you'd like to see it," said Ollie. He was seated next to Stan. Off to one side stood Vince Rossi, the GM's adviser and right-hand man. The GM beckoned with a wave of his hand. Ollie pulled up the full video of the batting tryouts and spun his laptop around. Vince and his boss leaned in.

Ollie said, "This is Montilla, now with the Athletics, and batting 295." After the at-bat, he said, "Chip Benson's next. Padres pulled him up this year to take over first."

Vince said, "That kid's been clobbering it."

"Hold on!" The GM hit pause and looked at Ollie. "Your guy is now pitching left."

Stan jumped in. "He's a switch-pitcher, boss. I sent the front office a sheet on him two weeks ago. Here's a copy." He tossed the paper on the desk.

The GM ignored it, his eyes fixed on the screen. "Give me a summary here."

"After Benson comes Gallego, who you've seen," said Ollie. "Then there's Jimmy Statsin with the Mariners, and Dylan Grainger, also with the Padres."

The GM looked to Vince who shrugged and said, "Serious talent."

"And this guy shut them all down?" asked the GM.

"Benson got a piece of one," said Ollie.

The GM leaned back again, hands clasped behind his head. "Problem is, I'm not looking for a novelty act."

Stan started to answer, but Ollie jumped in. "I'm not bringing you one. You need someone who can pitch late to more than one batter. A switch-pitcher is the answer. Gil can go after lefties and righties. He's not a freak show."

Stan couldn't contain himself. "Freak or not, the fans love him. He packs them in wherever he goes. That's always good for the game—and the organization. When I saw him pitch, I couldn't take my eyes off him. He's got that star quality."

The GM scanned Gil's sheet. "Appears he played everywhere but the majors."

"Almost," said Stan. And I made a couple of calls. The Aussies adore him. Hope to have him back if you pass. The Koreans think he's a national hero. People name their kids after him. Same goes wherever he played. Vince, look up switch-pitcher."

Vince looked it up on his phone. "He's everywhere. Let me check his website. Whoa. Lot of followers. Besides Australia and Korea, you have half of Europe, the Latinos, and on it goes until the Atlantic League. Helluva fan base for an unknown."

"He's only unknown here," said Ollie.

"And why do you think that is?" asked the GM, pedantically.

"He's different. And that's uncomfortable. It changes the game. But it doesn't make it wrong. In fact, I think he's your secret weapon. I'd stake my career on it."

The GM was stirred by the answer, but closed his eyes to hide it. "Who found him?"

"I coached him at Prescott High School."

"Aha! So this is your pet project. For old time's sake."

Ollie sighed heavily, swallowing his ire. "I'm here to bring you a viable contender."

The GM zeroed in on Stan through squinted, steely eyes. "How did you get on him? Through Ollie?"

"Huh-uh. JJ Jaggard spotted him."

The GM's eyebrows raised with interest. "That makes a difference. I'll have to give him a call. Get his take."

"He's outside."

"You asked him here?"

"Nope. He requested it."

The GM frowned. "Get him in here, Vince."

After JJ joined them, the GM said, "It's been awhile, JJ. So why I should be looking at this guy."

JJ looked at Stan and Ollie's dour expressions and chuckled. "I'm sure they've made it clear. But they work for you, and I don't. So I'll cut to the quick. Guys like Gil only come around once in a blue moon. Maybe once in a generation of players."

"Enough of the accolades. What's he pitch?"

"Depends on which arm," said JJ with a sly smile. "But overall, he's a junk dealer. Fastball's only for show. But he's got everything else in the book, including a lights-out knuckleball from the right. My guess is if you drop the correct sign, he'd throw you the kitchen sink. But it's more than that. He reads batters. Knows what to pitch from their swing, stance, hell, even their mood. And it works. He's pulling a 1.56 ERA over eight years, that's year-round ball, against players who are now beating up your D-backs."

The GM was frustrated. "That's all great, but the majors is a different animal."

"Not to Gil Hayes. He's going to make it to the show with or without you. In fact, I've already put out some feelers and have at least three teams who are interested right now. Including the Dodgers."

Ollie jumped to his feet. "JJ! What the hell?!"

"Sorry, Ollie. But you want the best for Gil, as do I. And I know he's got his heart set on the D-backs, homegrown boy and all. But I don't care. And there's no time to waste. He's money in the bank. Whoever misses out gets the short straw. Just the way it is."

The GM was at a loss, uncertain of what to do. JJ sensed this and pounced. "By the way, if someone hasn't already mentioned it, he's the best damn bunter I ever saw. Anywhere you want to put it. And he usually gets his base, even when it's a sac." He started for the door then turned back. "He's real fast."

"For a pitcher," said the GM.

"For anyone. He's clocking 29.2 feet per second right out of the box. In case you haven't kept up on it, the league average is 27. So that puts him up there with Dyson, Trout, Gordon, and few other slouches. So in a pinch, he's a cinch for DH. Oh, yeah, and he can steal. See you around." And he was gone.

The GM sat staring at Gil's sheet, his fingers massaging his temples, weighing the pros and cons. Vince whispered in his ear. "Arizona born, switch-pitcher—the fan appeal alone is enough to give him a try. No matter which way the season swings, we'll fill more seats. Other teams found that out with Venditte."

The GM nodded slowly and finally lifted his eyes to Ollie. "If I do this, I'll want to try him out in the minors before we get him on the expanded roster."

"It's still possible. But we're running out of time. Aces only have a few regular games to go unless we make the playoffs, which is looking iffy, at best." With a wry smile, he added, "Given all the pitchers you've stolen from us."

Abruptly, the GM shot to his feet. "Okay, we'll give him a try. He's unrestricted, right? So it should be quick and simple. Get him on the phone."

"He's got an agent," said Stan.

"What? He's a nobody!"

"Yeah, well, he's also got fans in high places. Name is Danny Kane."

"Whoop-de-doo," said the GM disgustedly. "Never heard of him. It'll be a pushover."

"He's Abe Scally's protégé."

"Are you kidding me? Why would Scally be backing this guy?"

Stan shrugged. "Like JJ said, he's a hot commodity."

"So it appears!" grumbled the GM. "You got a contact number?"

"He's outside."

"Of course he is! Why wouldn't he be?!"

"Sorry. We thought, just in case—"

"Yeah, yeah, get out of here! And send him in!"

Stan scooted out the door, dodging bullets. As Ollie started out, the GM said, "Is it true he always wanted to be with the D-backs?"

Ollie shrugged. "Grew up in Skull Valley. He needed some kind of dream, who wouldn't?"

The GM shook his head in defeat. With a wry grin, he said, "Thanks Ollie."

Ollie winked. "You're going to owe me more than that." He walked into the waiting room, his face stony. He looked at Danny seated next to JJ and Stan. After a well-timed pause, he broke a smile. "You're up."

"Seriously?!" asked Danny jumping to his feet.

"Don't sell him short," said Stan.

"Not a chance. Before I took off last night, Abe spent an hour prepping me."

"Yikes," said JJ. "I pity the poor guy in there."

Ollie laughed. "And nice going, JJ. The ploy worked like magic. I couldn't have done it better myself."

"You're right, you couldn't," said JJ, snickering. "But, like I said, I have the knack. It's all in the timing. Have to make them believe there's a clock ticking. No exec wants to go down in history being the one who passed on the next Greg Maddux. It's a real downer at cocktail parties."

"Gil's that good, isn't he?" asked Danny.

"You better believe it. So go get him in the show. It's about time."

Top of the 9th

I'M IN! I SIGNED A MAJOR LEAGUE CONTRACT and it's a day I'll never forget. I was out in the vacant lot showing Tyro how to throw a sinker. My lovely Jasmine was brave enough to be acting as our catcher. For the past week, everyone had been acting all gentle-like to me. Course, I knew right off what was up. They were feeling sorry for me, figuring my chance at being signed was over. I don't know why, but I was still holding out hope. Besides that, I knew if it didn't happen this year, I would keep on getting on until it did.

Anyway, there I was showing Tyro the correct arm angle and slot, and he was wailing about how his arm wouldn't work that way when Manny came tearing across the field. I thought he might keel over and die before he made it to us. He was wheezing and panting so much he couldn't get a word out.

We all waited patiently until he blurted out that Danny called. He tried to get ahold of me, but as usual I didn't have my phone. So he called Manny and told him the news. I just about passed out on the mound. With Jasmine kissing me and Tyro screaming in my ear, I thought I'd died and gone to heaven.

Then Manny tells me I need to get to Phoenix that very day. Seems they first had to officially get me on the forty-man roster so I could then be on the September expanded roster which would make me eligible to play in the post-season if the D-Backs got that far. It's all confusing, but bottom line, I had to get a move on. I needed to sign a bunch of papers in Phoenix, then fly to Reno that night to play with the Aces until the end of their season.

Everybody got real quiet, because none of us owned a car. Billy has one but he was gone fishing. I don't know how I thought of it, but I ran to my room, grabbed my phone and rang up Balrog. I told him I needed a lift pronto, and he jumped on it.

He and three other fellas showed up not more than a half hour later. I hopped on the back of his hog with my suitcase and off we went. We were burning up the road until we closed in on Phoenix.

Miles earlier, I had seen a large cloud, and thought nothing of it. As we neared the city, it was apparent that was no normal cloud. It's what desert folks call a haboob, which is a fancy word for a giant dust storm. I yelled to Balrog we should sit it out, but he wouldn't hear sense. He just revved it up and plowed into that damn thing. Well, he was game, but the hog wasn't. The dust clogged up the bike and it stalled right on the side of the highway.

The other three bikes were doing okay, though, so he swapped with one of his boys and off we went. By the time we made it, however, we were down to the last bike and it was sputtering and heaving the rest of the way. I don't even know how we survived with visibility at zero. Balrog and I stumbled into the D-Backs office just blanketed in dust. I think the lady receptionist was about to call the cops we were such a sight. Danny was waiting for us, though, and came to the rescue.

I rushed upstairs and went into a fancy office about three times the size of my apartment, and way better furnished. I met the big boss and he's a real swell guy. He was mighty impressed at the effort I'd put in getting there and I told him I always do everything one hundred percent. He sure liked that.

Anyway, I signed my name so many times my hand started cramping the way it did when I was a kid at school. Afterwards, Danny rushed me out to the airport. But we needn't have hurried, because all the planes were grounded due to the haboob. We stayed in a hotel that night and took off the next day.

By then, I'd developed a stubborn cough from all the dust I'd breathed in, so by the time I hit Reno I was in no shape to pitch. As we waited out my cough in the hotel room, Danny explained the contract. He seemed real disappointed with what he had managed, but when he told me how much money I was to get, my eyes nearly popped out of their sockets. Heck, I'm getting more for playing a month of ball then I did my whole time overseas.

But he was still frustrated, saying he wasn't looking for money. He wanted to get me a contract beyond this season. But the big boss wouldn't hear of it. He'd rather throw cash at me then commit to a long-term deal. Danny said that meant I might only be a major-leaguer for a month or so, and that would be it.

Well as I looked at my buddy so glum when he should be happy, I knew I had to cheer him up. That's when I told him my motto: It's not what they say, it's how you play. I explained that he had nothing to worry about. Now that I was here, the majors weren't going to get shy of me that easy. I was fixing to tear it up so bad in September the D-

Backs would be begging to sign me up again. Just like I predicted way back when.

And that did it. That old Danny grin just spread across his face wiping away any grief. I was relieved to see it. It's no fun celebrating when you got to do it alone.

It took three days for me to get that gunk out of my lungs, and by then, the Aces had been eliminated and their season was over. I guess the boss man in Phoenix was not too happy. He wanted to try me out before I hit the bigtime. Coach Denning, however, thought it was funny. After all I'd been through, I ended up being one of only three players in the 21st century who went from nowhere straight to the majors.

And that's where I am now. So far, I've been living up to my end of the bargain. Everybody told me things would be different once I faced pros, but they seem just as confused by what I throw as the hitters did wherever I've played. My pitching coach says it's because they don't have any tape on me. No way to research. He says I'm just in a grace period. Not sure what that means, but it sounds religious, and not being of the persuasion, I've chosen to ignore it.

The D-backs are making quite the stir around the league, and I can see why. We got a great bunch of guys, and they took to me real well, especially when I showed them how I cook. I rented an apartment for the time being. I'm so used to living with host families, it feels a little strange. But it's real big, so I can fix supper for almost half the team at a time.

Truth is, I can hardly believe where I am. I've been fighting for it so long, and now that it's here, it's hard to describe. I told Manny that very thing over the phone and he passed on a quote by a famous teacher named Alcott. It goes, "Success is sweet and sweeter if long delayed and gotten through many struggles and defeat."

That teacher must have written that with me in mind, because right about now it's feeling real sweet indeed, brother. Real sweet. The only thing that would be finer is if I can help my beloved team make it into October. And that's exactly what I'm fixing to do. Then they'll never be able to get rid of me.

Chapter 25

"THERE'S THE THROW TO FIRST AND HE'S OUT! Two down and one to go!" cried Steve, the play-by-play announcer for the Diamondbacks. "Can you believe what we're seeing, Bob?"

"Frankly, no! When we first saw Gil Hayes appear seemingly out of nowhere, I never would have imagined this."

"What surprises you most about him?"

"Well, honestly, he doesn't look like a pitcher. He's not that tall, doesn't have that imposing figure on the mound—"

"And let's not forget he throws with both arms!"

"Exactly! Nothing about him is what we think of as normal. But there's no denying, whatever he's doing is working. I've also been very impressed with his bunting skills. The rest of the pitchers in the game should take lessons."

"Unless the MLB adds the universal DH next year, then they won't have to."

"True. But it'd be a real shame. I like having pitchers hit."

"Turn it up," barked Manny.

"You need to get a hearing aid, old man!" shouted Tyro over the blaring volume. But he dutifully hit the remote and cranked it up a little more. The apartment was packed to capacity. Along with Manny and Tyro, Jasmine was there with Billy and the entire Redskins team.

"If he does this, we're going to need tickets!" cried Tyro.

"Already got them," said Manny. "I had a hunch."

"Me, too," said Billy. "Along with half the tribe. I hope he pulls it off."

"He'll do it," said Jasmine. "He promised me."

"Quiet!" yelled Tyro.

"You know, Bob," continued Steve. "I don't know if I've ever seen such a crazy wild-card race. Two weeks ago, the D-backs were five back, hoping to squeak into the second spot. But if Gil Hayes pulls off this miracle, their regular season record will be one win over the Nationals, giving them home-field advantage in the one-game playoff. It's been a real rollercoaster, and Arizona needed help from other teams above them. But the stars have aligned and here they are."

"And it's not the offense that's been getting it done, partner. They've provided just enough runs for a lead, then left it up to their new late reliever and closer Gil Hayes to finish it out. This will be the sixth game in a row he's had to save the game with only a one-run lead. And he has to do it against the Rockies at Coors Field. Sure, they're out of the running this year, but they're still the Rockies."

"And it's still Coors Field! And here we go, last man standing, and he happens to be hitting 310 for the season."

Tucker, Mandy and Alice sat shoulder to shoulder on the very edge of the couch. Skip was sprawled on the floor peering intently at the TV.

"In case he does do it," said Mandy, voice quivering. " Did you get tickets?"

"Of course," said Tucker. "Last week."

"That early?," asked Alice. "How did you know?"

"Gil said he didn't want everyone to have to travel far. Good enough for me."

"SSHHH!" demanded Skip.

"Batter backs off the plate," Steve announced. "I think he's a little confused. As a lefty, he figured Hayes would pitch left. But he's going with his right arm."

"Maybe he's thinking that wicked knuckleball will do the trick. He throws that about 40% of the time with his right arm. I'm still getting used to saying that. This switch-pitcher is a new animal to me."

"Well, get used to it, if he pulls this off, he's going to be around for quite some time. Okay, here we go. Hayes is set, and the abbreviated windup, and, strike one!"

"Good on ya, G-Man!" hollered Liam, now a strapping young man. Noah's living room was crammed with the entire Rangers team and several players from the ABL. Noah was in the back, pacing.

"Did you notice that, Bob?" asked Steve. "The pitch was clearly a knuckleball, like you called, but the catcher didn't drop any sign."

"I've been watching that over the last few games, and I think it's safe to say Hayes is the one calling the pitches, not the other way around. Not sure how they're doing it."

Noah yelled, "You gotta watch his shoulders and how many times he touches his cap, mate! That's how we used to do it!" Everyone howled, then Liam hushed them for the next pitch.

"Ooh! Foul ball. Just got a piece of that one. What the heck was that pitch, BB?"

"I have absolutely no idea! Like a lot of his pitches, they're a mixture of things. He's got a slurve, a cut changeup, and one that looks like a hybrid splitter forkball. What do you call that? A splork?"

"Works for me! Either way, the Rockies are down to their last strike. The Mets, Brewers and, in particular, the Nationals have all lost today. So this is it! For the wild-card home-field advantage."

Danny and JJ were seated near third base. Danny could barely keep still, hands twitching, knees bouncing. Even the seasoned scout was keyed up. Danny looked to him for reassurance, and JJ grinned, giving him the thumbs-up. It did not, however, help to subdue the fluttering butterflies in his stomach.

Ollie Denning was also feeling the strain. Due to his relation with Gil, he was asked to sit in the dugout. The manager figured if Gil needed a pep talk, he might know the magic words. But Ollie was so anxious he couldn't even stop his own jitters, much less offer words of wisdom.

Unlike his supporters, Gil was ice calm. He leaned forward, staring into home plate, mind searching for the correct pitch, senses studying the posture and demeanor of the batter. The last pitch had been close. The man was zeroing in on his slow stuff. He leaned back, touched his cap, tossed the ball twice up and down, then slapped it into his glove. It was his new sign for the fastball, and he was sure the catcher thought he was nuts. His fastball was hittable, especially from the right. Unless the batter didn't expect it. And Gil was sure he didn't.

At that moment, he had no idea how many people across the world were watching him. He did not realize what an indelible mark he had made over the years. As he got set, he could not imagine how much this meant to fans he had never met. He cleared his mind and threw.

"He froze him!" screamed Steve. "An 85-mph fastball right down Broadway and he just stood there and watched it go by! Diamondbacks win and they're going to the postseason! Unbelievable. And no doubt we owe this one to G-Man!"

Later, in the clubhouse, the sportscasters riddled Gil with questions.

"Gil! You've played everywhere in the world. Which country are you most fond of?"

"Without a doubt, Czechoslovakia."

"Why there?"

Gil grinned. "Well, I always wanted people to say I had a checkered past."

There was a beat, then everyone cracked up, none more than Gil who loved his own jokes.

"Gil! The way things have been going, you might be called on to close out another tight game. Does that make you nervous?"

Gil's face turned stony. "I'll tell you a little secret not many people know. The only time in life I'm not nervous is when I'm on the mound."

Just the way he said it made everyone in earshot frightened for the batters who would soon face him.

"Why did you decide to become a switch-pitcher?"

"Well, I was born with two arms and I figured it was a waste to use only one. Second, every once in a while, the game of baseball needs a little shaking up. That's what I aim to do."

In the back of the room, near the manager's office, the GM nodded slowly, realizing the rare gift that had dropped in his lap. Remembering the old, almost forgotten reason why he had dedicated his life to baseball. He looked over at the team's manager.

"Who are you looking at to start the wild-card game?"

"Not sure. We're down to rookies. We'll have to look at the matchups, and—"

"I want him," said the GM pointing at Gil.

"But he's never started!" said the manager. "And what if we need him as a closer?"

The GM shook his head. "You're looking at it through a magnifying glass. It's bigger than that. Win or lose, that kid is going to make history. And I'll be damned if I'm going to be the one to stand in his way. Put him in."

Chapter 26

GIL SENSED THERE WAS A PROBLEM the minute he walked into the clubhouse. The normal pre-game chatter suddenly vanished, eyes averted. He hadn't seen it coming, but it didn't surprise him. As he made his way to his locker, he wondered how to proceed. He had barely suited up, however, when the matter was brought to a head by "Jimbo," the D-backs' catcher and one of the few old-timers on the team.

The stocky player slammed his locker and spun to the others. "What the hell is this? You're not even going to say hello to the guy who's responsible for getting us into this game?! I think we owe him some gratitude."

One of the power hitters, "Raffy," stepped forward. "I got nothing against him. But he's never even started a game!"

Another shouted, "And he's closed six straight! With only two days off. How long can he keep it up?"

Jimbo didn't have a chance to argue, because Gil stood up and everyone went quiet. He spied the manager in his office, peering through the glass, wondering if he should intervene, yet knowing it best to have the team work it out on their own.

Gil pointed at him, "That man in there decided I was the right guy to start this game. I don't know how he knew, but I can tell you he's one smart fella. And that's not being cocky. It's true I haven't started a game in the big leagues, but I've been a starter most of my life. Sure, my arms are a little tired, but I know what it takes to do the innings. Most important, I know how big this game is to you guys. All season long, you've been scrapping and clawing, and you deserve this one. I've been preparing for this moment all my days. Can't guarantee I'll win it for you, but I promise one thing, I'll be out there pitching like it's the last big league game of my life. Because it might well be."

A chill went through the room. All the players understood. It's not easy getting into the show. And it's a whole lot tougher staying there.

"And let's be clear, Jimbo's wrong," he continued. "You don't owe me anything. I'm only here because of you. Make no mistake about that."

Everyone was transfixed, not sure how to respond. Gil understood. He knew what made ballplayers tick. They were his brothers. And he knew they were scared, unsure of everything but the desire to win. He grinned and the tension eased.

"I will make one small request, though."

"What's that?" asked Raffy.

"I sure could use some runs this time around."

After a brief pause, everyone cracked up, slapping their thighs, banging their lockers, and generally raising the roof. Raffy stepped up to Gil and slapped him on the back. "Consider it done, G-Man."

"Good evening ladies and gentlemen! This is Frank Larsen and my partner Dean "Professor" Harroway. Welcome to the National League Wild Card Game between the Washington Nationals and the Arizona Diamondbacks! I've just been informed this is shaping up to be the most-viewed Wild Card Game since its inception in 2012. And it's no secret why. For the first time in major league history, a switch-pitcher is starting a post-season game. To make it more interesting, he's a rookie, having just been picked up out of obscurity a few days before September as an amateur free agent. So, first question, Professor, have the Diamondbacks lost their minds?"

"Well, it's only fair to say Gil Hayes may be a rookie in this league, but he's pitched about everywhere the game is played. So, he's no babe in the woods. And his overall ERA is eye-popping. As far as being chosen as the starter in the biggest game of the season, well, rumor has it the decision came from the very top. So the responsibility lies with the GM, and one look at the stands tells me if he is crazy, it's like a fox. The place is packed to the gills and the fans are as geared up as I've ever seen."

"You've got that right. Though Hayes is a newcomer, he's quickly become a fan favorite. Supporters throughout the stadium are waving G-Man banners and chanting his name. Now, that's bigtime! And so is the cheer that just erupted as he jogs onto the field for his pre-game warm-up. We're in for a treat, Professor. Apparently, he is quite the juggler, and likes to entertain the crowd before games."

"Makes perfect sense. If you're going to use both arms what better way to warm them up? I tried it once, but couldn't keep more than one ball in the air."

"Better than me! You'll notice he's wearing number 36. When he first came up, he asked for 15, but it was unavailable. But you'll see he's wearing an armband with 15 on it. Our partner, Judy, asked him about it earlier, and here's what he had to say."

On the spot reporter, Judy, is standing next to Gil pointing at his armband. "This here represents unfinished business."

"Can you explain what you mean by that, Gil?" asked Judy.

"Sure can. Number 15 was worn by a lady named Rose. She was a great ballplayer, and she was on a mission, just like me. She never succeeded, so I'm here to finish the job—for both of us."

Frank said, "Well, I guess that answers it. Except I've never heard of this Rose lady. Still somewhat of a mystery."

"Not the only one regarding this young man. I talked to my good friend and color analyst for the D-backs, "BB" Brenly, and he said he wasn't always quite sure what pitches Hayes was throwing! And that from a world-class catcher!"

"And the real heart of the matter is he's pitching with both arms! He's only the third one in the modern era. Why do you think that is Professor?"

After a sigh, he said, "It's obvious, but nobody wants to admit it. Baseball has always been slow to adopt anything new. People believe it disrupts the integrity of the game. I must admit, I've fallen afoul of that attitude. But let's face it, when a rule is changed, the players have to adapt. Likewise, baseball should adapt to the people who play the game. And my guess is that's what Hayes' mission is. To show us lunkheads how to deal with reality, like it or not."

"I have to agree. I'm a dyed in the wool traditionalist too, but when you force yourself to think about it, what better edge can a pitcher have but throwing with both arms? And nobody's ever complained about switch-hitters."

"Good point, Frank."

"Sometimes I get lucky. Okay, we only have a short time before the first pitch, but we have a special guest today. So let's send it back down to Judy in the stands."

Judy is seated next to Tucker who's looking very nervous. They're in the 3rd base box seats adjacent to Arizona's dugout. In the background sit Alice, Mandy, Skip, Danny, JJ, Manny, Jasmine and Tyro.

"So, Tucker, you grew up with Gil, and you two are best friends, right?"

"Yep."

"Uh-huh, so it's safe to say you probably know him better than anyone."

"Reckon."

"And you've been kind of like his PR manager."

"I suppose."

"You've done a great job connecting his fans from around the world. In particular, you've arranged to have live video feeds from groups of his international supporters. We're going to take a look at some of them on the giant screen so our local fans can see just how many people in other countries are rooting for Gil. I'm hoping you'll be able to tell us what we're looking at."

"Here's the first one," said Judy. The JumboTron showed a group of cheering people packed inside a café, waving bottles of wine.

"That's the Italian Baseball Club, the Rangers Redipuglia," said Tucker. "But I don't pronounce it real well."

"I think you did very well! Here's another one. Oh my goodness!" The screen showed a baseball stadium jammed with frantically screaming people waving G-Man pennants.

"Those are the Koreans," said Tucker, grinning. "They just love my boy, They're broadcasting the game at one of their arenas. It sold out in thirty minutes."

The crowd in Chase Field are riveted to the screen, cheering on their fellow fans. "Let's look at one more," said Judy. A beach was seen filled with people hoisting beers and dancing. "Well, well, they certainly seem like a fun bunch!"

Tucker chuckled. "They're Aussies. They had to have a beach party because they couldn't find a place big enough to hold everybody. Look! There's Noah Walker in a hula skirt. He was the first coach who took a chance on Gil."

"Smart guy."

"You can say that again," said Tucker proudly.

Judy beckoned to the cameraman. "Can we pan over to right field. This is probably the largest single group we have in our stadium today. You can see many are wearing red headbands."

"That's the Pascua Yaqui Tribe out of Tucson," said Tucker. "Gil's an unofficial member. Like a mascot. That's why he wears the headband under his cap. They sure get a kick out of him."

"Obviously! And before we go. Behind us off to the left." The camera panned to a large swath of grizzled, leather-clad bikers. "I hate to ask, but what's up with that bunch?"

"Them? They're just the boys. Gil learned to pitch throwing against those galoots."

"You're kidding, right?"

"No ma'am."

"Wow. So I imagine after that, he's not afraid of anyone."

"Nope."

"Tucker, if you could sum it up. What is it about Gil that attracts people?"

He said with a grin, "Easy. He always delivers the goods. You'll see."

"I guess we will! Back to you, guys."

The Professor laughed. "I don't know about you Frank, but I wouldn't want to strike out any of those bikers. They might hold a grudge!"

"Amen to that! Well, Gil Hayes just keeps getting more fascinating. And we're about to see if he really can deliver the goods. First pitch coming up!"

Chapter 27

DESPITE THE HYPE, the D-backs manager was still not thrilled at having Gil start the game. He couldn't say anything to the GM, who was on cloud nine over the coverage this game was getting. But as he watched the Nationals' first batter step to the plate, he conferred with his bench coach.

"I want you to keep a close eye on his pitch count."

"Which arm?" asked the bench coach wryly.

"I'm serious. In my mind, he's our opener. First sign of trouble and I'm yanking him. This game is too important."

"Your call," said the coach, wanting to relieve himself of any responsibility.

"That's right," said the manager through clenched teeth.

The Nationals had done their homework on Gil, and stacked the line-up with switch-hitters. There were four, including a reserve bench player. The Venditte Rule had changed over the years, now requiring the pitcher to signal which arm he was using before the at-bat. This gave a switch-hitter a partial advantage as they could choose which side to hit from after the pitcher had declared.

Initially, however, it made little difference. The top half of the first inning saw three groundball outs in as many pitches. As Gil jogged toward the dugout, the crowd roaring with glee, the bench coach leaned into the manager with a grin.

"That's a total of three. Two from the right and one from the left. You think he's still good to go for the second inning?" The manager scowled at him.

Unlike many pitchers, Gil didn't go off by himself when he wasn't pitching. He was at the railing, watching the action, egging on his team, and often giving players tips before going to bat. He was very adept at reading the opposing pitchers, and his advice was actively sought out.

True to their word, his teammates put up two runs in the bottom of the first. Many pitchers relaxed with a lead, but Gil never let up. He knew how fickle the game could be.

At the top of the second, as he walked to the mound, his mind went through what he knew of the upcoming batters. He had done his normal research the day before, but what he mostly used was the knowledge he gleaned right before the game. He once heard Greg Maddux always came early to the park and watched the opposing team do batting practice. Gil religiously followed suit. The video on players only showed what they had done on previous days. Gil was looking to see how they felt on the day he would pitch to them. This practice made him a dangerous adversary.

Nevertheless, his second inning did not go as smoothly as the first. His style was to pitch to contact. His groundball percentage was fifty percent—the MLB leader was at fifty-four. The problem is no matter what shift is put on, some balls get through. Due to a couple that did,

Gil and his teammates had to fight to finally get the first two outs and clear the bases.

It appeared he would cruise through the last batter, when a curveball hung and it was knocked over the right field fence. Gil was furious with himself, and erased the next batter with three straight pitches. But his pitch count had shot up. He wasn't worried, but he dearly wanted that run back.

In the bottom of the second, the sixth man in the D-backs lineup went down on strikes. The seventh, Perez, a speedster, hit a soft line drive and turned it into a double by a hair. Jimbo was the eighth man up, and though an excellent catcher, was no hitter. He popped-up on his first pitch and tossed his bat in disgust.

Gil was starting out of the on-deck circle when he suddenly retraced his steps, beckoning to the manager at the top of the dugout.

"Skipper," said Gil. "This situation recalls something I heard old "Popeye" Zimmer used to talk about."

The manager shook his head with irritation. "Just go try and bunt for base, Gil. Without getting hurt!"

"No problem, chief. But here's my point. Dickson on third has bad knees, right? And their catcher is a third-stringer. Now Perez can fly like the wind. I'm no slouch either, as you know. So I'm thinking if we put the squeeze on, it's a sure thing to get Perez home."

The manager opened his mouth to argue, but his trusted bench coach grunted in agreement. The manager narrowed his eyes, tacitly admitting it was a good call. But he wasn't sure if Gil could pull it off.

"Play only works if you sell it."

"Don't you worry, skipper. I'll make sure my boy gets in."

With a curt nod, the decision was made. Gil smiled and the manager growled.

"What could Hayes be talking about?" asked Frank in the press booth. "The best he can do is move Perez to third."

The Professor chuckled. "Well, I picked up a few tidbits about G-Man, and he's an expert bunter, with speed like Perez. Maybe they're up to some hijinks."

A complex series of signs went from the third base coach to Perez, who nodded, nonchalantly. Gil stepped into the batter's box. He spit on the first two pitches which were strikes, but not what he was looking for. The third pitch, however, he bunted low, medium slow toward the third baseman and took off. Perez shot away from second.

"Wait a minute," cried Frank. "Perez is rounding third! What's he doing?"

The Nationals were clearly dumfounded. The catcher and third baseman were chasing the bunt as the shortstop ran to cover third base. Dickson came up with the ball, but by the time he turned to throw to third, Perez was zooming past, heading to home. As Dickson spun, he spied Gil rounding first on his way to second—forcing his hand. Too risky to try and get Perez only a few feet from home. He was down to one play. He fired the ball to the second baseman who hung Gil up between the bases. Gil danced around making sure the run was across, then gave himself up.

"And that's the squeeze play!" said the Professor. "A delayed suicide squeeze, to be exact. Perez acts like he's happy with third but then just keeps running. Hayes played it perfectly by rounding first, forcing Dickson into a decision. By the time he chose, the run scores before the runner is tagged out. You trade an out for a run! Beautiful."

"And sneaky!" added Frank.

"That's baseball!" said the Professor. "But this is no normal pitcher. That play only works with elite speed."

The bench coach sidled up to the D-backs manager. "He's at 27. About an even split. You think this is a good time to pull him, skipper?" he deadpanned.

The manager ignored him, still a little stunned, his head slowly shaking back and forth as he replayed the moment in slow motion. It had taken but a few seconds, but he knew he would remember it forever.

The next three innings showed Gil at his finest. He was settled in and using everything in his arsenal. "These Nationals just don't have an answer for G-Man, Professor," said Frank. "What's his secret?"

"Well, the game has evolved. Especially with pitching. Everything's harder, faster, and the hitters have become accustomed. Used to be guys threw their sliders at 75. Now, they're at 90. The batters have to swing quicker to catch up. And, suddenly, they're facing a junk master like Hayes, and they can't make the adjustment."

"I've noticed he's also changing his delivery almost every pitch."

"Yeah. It's like he's channeling Vic Raschi, the great Yankees pitcher of the 40's and 50's. Lots of deception. No pitch the same. Sidearm, overarm, quick pitch, varying ball speed, going in and out to keep them on the rocking chair. There's so many patterns they're not sure what to focus on. And watch how he changes where he lines up on the rubber. This creates multiple arm angles so his pitches look like they're moving more than they are. Very cagey."

"And with all of that, he's putting the ball right where he wants it every time."

"He's a Wiffle ball pitcher. Pinpoint accuracy. And to make it even more difficult to face him, his pitch selection is designed to deceive the batter's eye by constantly changing the position of his pitches. I'm also impressed by how he shapes his breaking balls. He has a knack of seeing the spin on the ball and recognizing how it affects the arc and speed. If I didn't know better, I'd think he was a ten-year veteran."

"Well, if he keeps going the way he is, it's going to be a tough night for Washington."

By the top of the sixth, the score held 3-1. Gil's pitching was masterful, but the D-backs were also being outpitched by the Nationals' pitcher, who had settled in. The first man up hit a dribbler to right field and was thrown out. The second struck out on three straight knuckleballs. Next up was the guy who had hit the home run, Rick Schuler.

He and Gil quickly locked horns and the count went full. Then Schuler started swinging at everything, fouling balls one after the other. Gil was pitching him right-handed and the pitch count was racking up. The deadlock continued until the 12th pitch. Gil was frustrated. An idea came to mind, and he waved Jimbo in for a conference.

Frank said, "This is G-Man's first mound visit. You can tell he's a little flustered. He doesn't want to hang another curveball like the one Schuler hit out of here."

Jimbo listened patiently to Gil's suggestion, then couldn't help but start laughing and slapping his knee. It was contagious and Gil joined in. Schuler looked angrily to the umpire who started toward the mound to break up the conversation.

"What was that all about?" asked Frank. "Looks like Gil cracked a joke or something. A heck of a time to be kidding around."

"Maybe he's got something up his sleeve," said the Professor.

Jimbo returned to his position, still shaking his head and chuckling.

"Yuck it up now," said Schuler. "Because after I clobber this thing, you'll have nothing to laugh about."

Jimbo looked up at him, a sparkle in his eyes. "Better get ready. It's coming like lightning."

"Yeah, right," said Schuler. "This guy's got no fastball." Yet, he thought about it. Maybe Hayes had been sandbagging, and was now going to bring the heat.

Behind his mitt, Gil gripped the seam with three fingers over top. He cocked his arm and threw. The ball flipped off the three fingers, creating backspin and sailing high, attaining an arc of 25 feet. Schuler started to swing, stopped, started again, froze, and finally swung hard. A second later—coming almost straight down—the ball crossed the plate at 45 mph.

"Strike three!" boomed the umpire, ringing him up with his signature flourish.

Schuler's mouth gaped. "What the hell was that?!"

"An education," said the umpire. "Go sit down."

Schuler flicked his bat away and kicked dirt onto home plate—a mortal sin. Before he was ejected, his manager rushed out and dragged him back to the dugout.

The Professor was on his feet. "Gil Hayes officially has nerves of steel! After all that, he gets him with an Eephus pitch! The ultimate hanging curveball!"

"Is that even legal?" asked Frank.

"You betcha! "Rip" Sewell created it after he injured with buckshot during a hunting accident and had to reinvent himself. In 1943, he won twenty games throwing that pitch. And a lot of others have used it. Al McBean, Yu Darvish, even Satchell Paige. It's got a lot of nicknames: moon ball, parachute, Bugs Bunny curve. But it comes down to one thing. Schuler is back in the dugout and we're going to the bottom of the sixth!"

Arizona's bats remained cold, and the inning was quickly over. In the top of the seventh, Gil's pitches began to lose their crispness. He was only human, and the innings pitched in games leading to this were starting to take their toll. Tucker sensed it in the stands. Jimbo felt it from behind the plate. And in the dugout, the manager eyed his pitch count and was not happy.

Gil had to pitch out of trouble after a line drive got through and put a man on second. He felt fortunate by the time he recorded three outs and jogged slowly back to the bench. The manager wanted to have a talk with him, but Gil was up second, and the meeting never took place.

Jimbo batted first and hit a slow roller and was thrown out. When Gil stepped up, the Nationals held a grudge, determined not to let him bunt for base. They used a dramatic shift, leaving only two men in the outfield and stacking the infield with five players. Gil studied the layout. He was tired, but up for the challenge.

On the second pitch, he squared up and chopped hard on the ball sending it straight down, ricocheting high into the air. He took off in a sprint and by the time the ball came to earth, he was safe at first.

"What a student of the game!" cried the Professor. "The Baltimore Chop. Usually it's an accident. But this was obviously intentional. That's what speed will do for you."

Unfortunately, the next two batters were unable to put wood on the ball and Gil was back on the mound for the top of the eighth. The Nationals smelled blood. They could see he was wavering and started their at-bats aggressively. Three straight hits ended as loud outs, but only exceptional plays in the outfield saved them from being homeruns.

When Gil hit the dugout, the manager immediately grabbed him and hustled him to the far end of the bench. The bench coach and Denning joined them.

"I think you've run out of gas, Gil," said the manager.

"You kidding, skipper? I got this," said Gil, with all the bravado he could muster.

"Give me the count," barked the manager.

The bench coach mumbled, "112."

"Yeah, but if you divide that by two, I'm looking good!"

The manager ignored him and turned to Denning. "You ever see him go this far? Does he have anything left?"

Denning stared at him. "The question is, do you have anyone in the bullpen with the same heart?"

The manager gnashed his teeth. His bullpen was a sore spot, and Denning just poured salt on the wound. He looked at Gil. "One mistake. You hear me? You let one guy on base, and I'm pulling you." He turned and walked away.

Gil looked at Denning. "Thanks."

"Don't thank me. Just go prove him wrong."

The D-backs were still stymied and Gil had little time to rest. He took the mound for the top of the ninth, digging deep to tap into his reserves. All adrenaline gone, he had to rely on pure guts.

He had a tough line-up coming to the plate. A lefty, a switch-hitter, and a righty. If it went further than that, a power hitter was cleanup. He started out from the left side to gain the edge, and it worked. It took five pitches, but the batter struck out. The switch-hitter batted right against Gil's left arm, giving him the advantage. He hit a slider on the second pitch. It looked like an easy out, but took a funny bounce and slipped under the mitt of the second baseman, putting the batter on first.

It was called an error, no fault of Gil's. He looked to the dugout. The manager was arguing with his bench coach. He waited for the hook, but it never came. He still had a little life. He switched his glove to his left hand and bent to touch the rubber, signifying he would pitch right to the righty, hoping for an edge.

He opted for a steady diet of knuckleballs. The count went 2-2. On the fifth pitch, the batter swung over the ball for an out—until the ball hit the dirt and careened away from Jimbo. The batter took off and crossed first before Jimbo could make a throw. He looked to Gil, shaking his head in agony over his error.

"That's the problem with the knuckleball," said the Professor. "It's great when it works, but it takes a great blocking catcher like Jimbo. He just got unlucky there."

Again, Gil looked to the dugout, but the manager was holding fast. None of the men on were his doing, and he would be allowed to go one more batter.

The next up was a power hitter, and no matter how hard Gil tried, he couldn't get him to bite on any of his breaking pitches. After seven tosses, the man walked. Bases loaded. One out.

The manager yelled to no one in particular, "I'm getting him out of there!"

He sprang out of the dugout and the first person who saw him coming was Tyro, leaning over the front rail, expecting this. Before the manager could take more than a couple steps, Tyro began chanting, "Leave him in!"

His shrill voice carried to the rows behind, and people immediately joined in. Like a wildfire, it spread throughout the stadium. The sound was deafening. Each step the manager took toward the mound it increased in volume. The crowd was on its feet, angrily waving him back. The JumboTron flashed shots of the international fans joining in. He started to lift his right arm to call in a right-handed reliever and the chants turned to passionate boos. He slowly pivoted, taking in the amazing sight. His eyes landed on Gil who grinned sheepishly and shrugged.

For the rest of his days, he would never be able to relay why he did what he did at that moment. Perhaps it was fear of the fans turning on him, or maybe he decided they knew better. Either way, he spun on his heels and marched back to the dugout.

A giant cheer exploded. The crowd, flexing their muscles having just influenced the game, began chanting, G-Man. Over and over it went. The umpire waved in the next batter, and still it continued, larger and larger, until the stadium literally pulsated with the thundering noise.

Gil lifted his cap to the audience, slowly taking them all in—forty-eight thousand five hundred and nineteen cheering for him. He waved his cap and they all waved back. It was a pristine moment, indelibly etched in his mind.

He replaced his cap and got down to business. The batter was the reserve man off the bench, another switch-hitter. He was, however, an oddball, in that he hit better against lefties from his left, and vice versa. Therefore, Gil knew no matter what side he pitched from, the hitter would opt to bat from the same side. He touched his left hand to the rubber, and the crowd hushed a bit, understanding the chance he was taking. As expected, the batter opted to hit left.

The first two pitches were balls. The crowd got a little quieter. The next two were clean strikes, and the audience held its breath. The fifth pitch resulted in a low-flying foul ball, heading just down from the D-backs' dugout. Gil took off in a sprint. He was far faster than either Jimbo or Raffy on third. If it could be caught, it would be up to him.

"Look at him go!" cried Frank. "But from our angle, it looks like that ball is going to fall into the stands. He better be careful."

Gil thought of nothing but catching the ball. His eyes zoning in on it, judging its trajectory, glove outstretched. A momentary flash in his mind warned him of the approaching wall, but it was too late. He only had time to reach out with his left hand as he slammed into the low wall and went down, the ball bounding into the stands. As one, the crowd gasped.

Gil's loved ones were just down from where he had landed. He heard Jasmine and Alice screaming. Then suddenly Tyro was leaning over the wall looking down at him.

The human mind is a strange beast. At times, it can think about things that seem out of place. At that moment, Gil wasn't thinking about what had happened, or whether he was injured. He could only think one thing—he needed to be pitching to that batter with his right arm. But there was nothing to be done. Except, maybe—

"G-Man! Are you alright?" asked Tyro leaning over the rail.

Gil grinned. Then winked.

Suddenly, his teammates surrounded him, helping him to his feet. The manager and trainer rushed up, followed by the home plate umpire. There was chatter coming from all sides, but Gil blocked it out. He was on a mission. He grasped his left forearm where it had hit the wall and winced.

The trainer immediately took the arm and started turning it this way and that. Gil dutifully clenched his teeth, betraying his pain.

"How does this feel, Gil?" asked the trainer.

"Peachy keen! Let's get back to it."

"Forget it," said the manager, turning to the umpire. "I need a new pitcher to finish out this at-bat. His left arm is done."

Gil blurted, "Then I'll finish him with my right arm, dammit! Venditte Rule allows for it. Tell him Ump, please! I can't quit like this!"

The umpire shrugged. "He's right. He's allowed to switch during an at-bat if an arm is injured. Clearly it is. So it's not going to be me who stops him from going on. But once it's done, no more pitching from the left."

The manager frowned. Gil said, "Please, skipper. One more."

"Can we have a few minutes here?" asked the manager.

The umpire nodded and walked back to the plate. In a huddle, the team moved back onto the field.

Alice was disconsolate. "My boy is hurt! He needs medical attention. They need to take him out." Jasmine tried comforting her, but she was thinking the same thing.

Tyro ran back to the group, all smiles. "He's faking. I just know it. He wanted to switch arms, and it's the only way he could do it."

Tucker asked, "Why do you say that?"

"Because Gil told me never to believe anything a pitcher tells you," said Tyro.

Tucker grinned. "That's Gil alright."

In the booth, Frank said, "Not sure what's going on down there, but the D-backs seem to be discussing more than if Hayes is going to pitch. A few of them just cracked up over something. What could possibly be so funny?"

Once Gil had revealed his ruse—much to the delight of his teammates—he said to the manager in serious tones, "Shift toward third, skipper. Ball's going that way. Raffy, you've got a cannon for an arm, so if you're too far away to tag your base, go straight home. Jimbo should still have time to go to second. The man on first is way slower than the guy at the plate."

"You're a sly devil, Gil," said the manager. "But he's a pull hitter, what makes you think the ball is going left."

"I'm coming with the screwball, skipper."

The manager nodded, seeing the ploy. Screwball from a right-handed pitcher should fade away from a batter lining up left. "What if he just switches to his right?"

"Rule don't allow for it. He's stuck where he is. It's worth a shot. If it doesn't work, we should at least get the second out. The bullpen can wrap up the last guy."

"Maybe," said Jimbo. "But I think it's now or never."

The manager shook his head in defeat. "Alright, you heard him. Put the shift on, and let's get these guys."

The huddle broke up, and everyone took their positions. When the manager of the Nationals sorted everything out, he argued that his batter should be allowed to switch, but all for naught. Rules are rules.

The crowd was on their feet, but not a sound could be heard as Gil stepped on the rubber. He stared out at home plate, no longer nervous over this batter. He was coming at him from the best side possible, and there was no hesitation.

The screwball did exactly as designed, fading away the last fifteen feet from the plate. The batter swung, clipping it to the left of the mound. Raffy took it on one bounce and fired a rocket to home. Jimbo tagged the plate on the force out and threw to second in plenty of time. 5-2-4 double play. Game over.

Pandemonium ensued. The Diamondbacks converged on Gil. They hoisted him up on Jimbo's shoulders and paraded him around the top of the mound.

He had become who he was born to be. King of the Hill.

Extra Innings

I AM OFFICIALLY IN THE HISTORY BOOKS! First switch-pitcher to pitch a complete game, and first to start a post-season game. It was only the Wild Card Playoff, but it's good enough for me. It was a crazy ordeal, and we won through a lot of luck, hard work, and a few tricks I had up my sleeve. After it was over, the people in the stadium didn't want to leave. It was like a gigantic block party, and I was the guest of honor, so to speak.

All my friends and family were there. Even the boys turned out. Of course, they can't go anywhere without getting into a little trouble. They were so geared up, they broke down a barrier so they could celebrate on the field and had to be carted away. But boys will be boys.

Anyway, after the game, the team didn't have much time to relish our win, because we had to hop on a plane and go play those darn Dodgers. We didn't fare so well in that series, and were promptly eliminated. But that's baseball. Love it or leave it. The good thing is, there's always next year.

It's strange being in the off-season. I haven't had many of those in my life. I told Billy I wanted to keep working, so I'd be busy. He thought I was nuts, now that I'm some big major-leaguer. But he agreed to let me come in and mingle with the patrons.

Oh, yeah. Jasmine said now that I reached my goal, it was alright for us to be together. So now we are officially sweethearts! I couldn't be luckier. We got us a big apartment in Tucson with a gigantic kitchen. We're always having people over so I can cook for them. And Tyro appointed me official coach of his team, so I can teach his boys how to play the game the right way. Life is real good.

Little Skip says he wants to be a switch-pitcher when he grows up, so when I visit Prescott, I've been showing him a few tricks and teaching him how to juggle. It's great being so close I can visit anytime I want. Tucker likes it, too. And mom, well she's never been happier.

I'm sure someday, a pitcher will come along and break my records. But that's okay, they're made to be broken. And I still may set some more along the way. Oh, I forgot to mention. After the season was over, the GM of the Diamondbacks had a meeting with Danny and was practically begging to have me stay part of the team. Just like I promised would happen when I started this whole thing.

Heck, I told Danny I'd play for free and he about had a heart attack, saying that's why I needed an agent. Apparently, their job is to wring out as much money as possible. He must be a pretty good one, because I'm locked in for two years and sitting pretty in hog heaven right about now. I don't even know what you're supposed to do with so much money. Jasmine says she'll think of something, so I'll let her worry about it.

The most important thing I've learned in this process is that no journey can be taken alone. It took a lot of people to get me where I needed to be. I owe them everything. For those of you who are thinking about chasing your own dream, remember to take help where it's offered. Don't ever turn your back on those who are living the journey right along with you. It's just as important to them as it is to you. And <u>mark my word</u>, they're the ones who are going to make sure you cross the finish line.

From the Author

I personally want to thank you for reading this book. I hope you enjoyed it. If so, please post a review at the site where you bought it.

If you'd like to read more of my books, check out the **Tinman Series**, my latest contribution to making the world a funnier place to live. Join this lovable gang of crooks as they tackle impossible heists, with hilarious results. The first two books, **Posse of Thieves** and **Shady Deal**, are available on Amazon. The third book, **Calling the Shots**, is soon to be released. Go to *www.crookbooks.site* for more details and a complete description. Also available is **Thieves Cookbook**, featuring twelve short stories with accompanying recipes and cooking tips from Tinman, the crook who cooks. It's a delicious mix of comedy, crime and cooking.

If you're looking for love, try **Love on the Lam**. This is a romantic comedy about two people who discover that crime doesn't pay, unless you're stealing someone's heart.3

Check out my blog at www.crookbooks.site/blog where you will also find interesting posts, free short stories and recipes.

Peace to all and long live laughter.

About the Author

Marc J. Reilly began entertaining people as a child actor. He graduated to directing and producing, and successfully founded two theater companies. He has worked in film as a cameraman, and director. For over two decades, he has worked as a freelance writer, while also writing several plays, books, and screenplays. He now concentrates his efforts to the writing of novels. He lives in Reno with the apple of his eye, Peg.

Made in the USA
San Bernardino, CA
25 March 2020